Cambridge Elements

Elements in Gender and Politics
edited by
Tiffany D. Barnes
University of Texas at Austin
Diana Z. O'Brien
Washington University in St. Louis

GENDER, ETHNICITY, AND INTERSECTIONALITY IN CABINETS

Asia and Europe in Comparative Perspective

Amy H. Liu
University of Texas at Austin

Roman Hlatky
University of North Texas

Keith Padraic Chew
Arizona State University

Eoin L. Power
University of Texas at Austin

Sam Selsky
University of Texas at Austin

Betty Compton
University of Texas at Austin

Meiying Xu
University of Texas at Austin

Shaftesbury Road, Cambridge CB2 8EA, United Kingdom

One Liberty Plaza, 20th Floor, New York, NY 10006, USA

477 Williamstown Road, Port Melbourne, VIC 3207, Australia

314–321, 3rd Floor, Plot 3, Splendor Forum, Jasola District Centre, New Delhi – 110025, India

103 Penang Road, #05–06/07, Visioncrest Commercial, Singapore 238467

Cambridge University Press is part of Cambridge University Press & Assessment, a department of the University of Cambridge.

We share the University's mission to contribute to society through the pursuit of education, learning and research at the highest international levels of excellence.

www.cambridge.org
Information on this title: www.cambridge.org/9781009570473

DOI: 10.1017/9781009570466

© Amy H. Liu, Roman Hlatky, Keith Padraic Chew, Eoin L. Power, Sam Selsky, Betty Compton, and Meiying Xu 2025

This publication is in copyright. Subject to statutory exceptionand to the provisions of relevant collective licensing agreements,no reproduction of any part may take place without the writtenpermission of Cambridge University Press & Assessment.

When citing this work, please include a reference to the DOI 10.1017/9781009570466

First published 2025

A catalogue record for this publication is available from the British Library

ISBN 978-1-009-57047-3 Hardback
ISBN 978-1-009-57043-5 Paperback
ISSN 2753-8117 (online)
ISSN 2753-8109 (print)

Additional resources for this publication at www.cambridge.org/liu_resources

Cambridge University Press & Assessment has no responsibility for the persistence or accuracy of URLs for external or third-party internet websites referred to in this publication and does not guarantee that any content on such websites is, or will remain, accurate or appropriate.

Gender, Ethnicity, and Intersectionality in Cabinets

Asia and Europe in Comparative Perspective

Elements in Gender and Politics

DOI: 10.1017/9781009570466
First published online: January 2025

Amy H. Liu
University of Texas at Austin

Roman Hlatky
University of North Texas

Keith Padraic Chew
Arizona State University

Eoin L. Power
University of Texas at Austin

Sam Selsky
University of Texas at Austin

Betty Compton
University of Texas at Austin

Meiying Xu
University of Texas at Austin

Author for correspondence: Amy H. Liu, amy.liu@austin.utexas.edu

Abstract: What explains patterns of representation – of women and ethnic minorities – in government cabinets? The authors argue governments diversify their cabinets when (1) a minority group – and it need not be ethnic – is sizable and can mobilize (political competition); and/or (2) the general population believes in and expects the inclusion of minorities (popular norms). The authors test their argument using original cabinet data from Asia and Europe (*N*=93) 1960–2015 and a controlled comparison of four case studies. They identify the gender and ethnicity of 91,000 country-year-minister observations – with consideration of the rank of their ministerial portfolio. They find evidence that in countries where there is political competition and/or popular norms, cabinets have fewer men from the hegemon ethnic group. However, this does not necessarily suggest minorities are holding portfolios of substantive prestige. This project offers a way to study intersectionality in democratic representation and political institutions.

Keywords: cabinets, ethnicity, gender, intersectionality, representation

© Amy H. Liu, Roman Hlatky, Keith Padraic Chew, Eoin L. Power, Sam Selsky, Betty Compton, and Meiying Xu 2025

ISBNs: 9781009570473 (HB), 9781009570435 (PB), 9781009570466 (OC)
ISSNs: 2753-8117 (online), 2753-8109 (print)

Contents

1 Introduction — 1

2 A Theory on Minorities in Cabinets — 12

3 Minorities and Cabinet Compositions — 25

4 Minorities and Portfolio Prestige — 42

5 Minorities in Cabinets in Four Cases — 56

6 Democracy and Cabinet Composition — 74

7 Discussion: What Next? — 77

References — 80

An online appendix for this publication can be accessed at www.cambridge.org/liu_resources

1 Introduction

When Singapore found itself suddenly independent in 1965, the first cabinet had ten ministers. Three were ethnic minorities: Othman Wok – an ethnic Malay – who was the Minister of Culture; S. Rajaratnam – the Foreign Affairs Minister – who was an Indian of Tamil ancestry; and Edmund Barker (Minister for Law), who was Eurasian – that is, someone of mixed European and Asian descent. The presence of ethnic minorities in the government was no fluke. The People's Action Party (PAP) – the party that controlled the government – had campaigned on a multicultural Singapore. This was a necessary – and the *only* feasible – position for countering the popularity of communism (Lee 1998). And since 1965 – as the PAP continues to govern with an authoritarian hand – Singaporean cabinets have always included multiple ethnic minorities (see Figure 1 – first panel).

Despite the presence of multiple ethnic minorities in the cabinets from the outset, the story is remarkably different when it comes to women. For almost forty years, until the mid-2000s with Lim Hwee Hua, there were no women in the Singaporean cabinets. Moreover, when there were women, they were almost always ethnic Chinese – the politically dominant ethnic group. It was not until 2018 that Singapore had its first ethnic minority woman in the cabinet (Indranee Rajah).

Contrast Singapore to Taiwan (second panel). As the Kuomintang (KMT) military dictatorship retreated from China to Taiwan in 1949, it took with it a government apparatus and an ethnic hegemon group. The first cabinet had *one* singular ethnic minority Taiwanese. The second ethnic minority minister joined in 1961. Starting in the mid-1970s, we see an increasing number of ethnic minorities in the cabinet, with many of them in prestigious portfolios. And then by 1988, we see gender minorities – from both the hegemon and minority ethnic groups – in the cabinet. In fact, the very first woman – Finance Minister Shirley Wang-jung Kuo – was an ethnic minority. Since 2000 – the year KMT lost power for the first time, thus marking Taiwan as a "democracy" – Taiwanese cabinets have continued to diversify to include aboriginal and nonbinary ministers.

These two cases – Singapore and Taiwan – highlight how *all* countries have cabinets. It is not a democracy-specific institution. Moreover, who holds the portfolios can vary drastically – both spatially and temporally. As we see in the first panel of Figure 2, the proportion of portfolios held by *double-hegemons* – men from the dominant ethnic group – has dropped over time. This eleven-point drop (from 0.86 to 0.75 in 2015) is consistent with Borrelli (2002), who argues there is an increasing expectation that governments should reflect the diversity

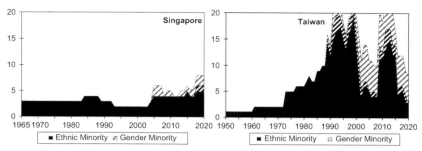

Figure 1 Number of Gender and Ethnic Minorities in Cabinets in Singapore and Taiwan

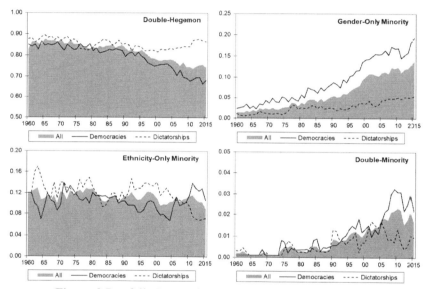

Figure 2 Portfolio Proportions by Each Group (1960–2015)

of their populations. The second panel shows that the proportions of *gender-only minorities* have steadily grown over time – from 0.01 in 1960 to 0.14 in 2015. Yet, the third panel illustrates that although the proportions for *ethnicity-only-minorities* are generally larger than that for *gender-only minorities*, they have remained largely constant over time at around 0.12. And finally, while *double-minorities* constitute the smallest proportion at any given time, we are seeing a twofold increase in their numbers (fourth panel). There is also substantial variation across and within regime types. Democracies tend to be more inclusive of minorities than autocracies, and this gap appears to be increasing over time. Yet, it was only recently that democratic cabinets began to include more ethnic minorities than authoritarian cabinets. And while authoritarian regimes continue to lag their democratic counterparts when it comes to gender representation, women have also assumed more cabinet positions in recent years.

Descriptive representation is important – whether it is about gender (Barnes and Holman 2020; Holman and Schneider 2018; Reingold 2008; Wolbrecht and Campbell 2007), ethnicity (Anthias and Yuval-Davis 1983; Guinier 1994; Hero and Tolbert 1995; Minta 2011; Preuhs 2005), *or the intersection of gender and ethnicity* (Brown 2014; Htun and Ossa 2013; Hughes 2011, 2016; Phillips 2021; Philpot and Walton 2007; Reingold, Haynie, and Widner 2020; Reingold, Widner, and Harmon 2020). When groups are descriptively represented, they exhibit higher levels of political efficacy (Atkeson and Carrillo 2007; Barnes and Burchard 2013; Lajevardi et al. 2024; Reingold and Harrell 2009; Sanchez and Morin 2011). Descriptive representation can mobilize minorities to vote (Griffin and Keane 2006; Hayes et al. 2024). Likewise descriptive representation can have downstream consequences on symbolic representation – the sense that the political system is representative of or "stands for" a given group (e.g., Hansen and Treul 2015: 957). In turn, symbolic representation can empower minorities in both the private and public sphere (Burnet 2009), spurring positive attitudes about intergroup interactions (Chauchard 2014). And, finally, descriptive representation may lead to substantive representation – the advancement of policy that benefits and corresponds with the interests of the group being represented (Atchison 2015; Bratton and Ray 2002; Cowell-Meyers and Langbein 2009; Pitkin 1967; Reyes-Housholder 2016).

Given the importance of descriptive representation – not just in the legislature but in all political institutions – we ask: **What explains cabinet compositions?** We argue **gender** and/or **ethnic minorities** gain positions in cabinets when the *double-hegemons* are constrained and must include a minority group. This constraint can manifest through two mechanisms that need not be mutually exclusive.

The first is through **political competition**. First, when a minority group is sizable – and note that the minority group need not be ethnic – it can mobilize. This mobilization can happen on the streets and/or at the ballot box. The efficacy of mobilization is a function of institutional context. Open and regularized channels of competition facilitate mobilization; conversely, closed and informal channels preclude it. As such, in noncompetitive political arenas, minority groups have to rely on nonelectoral means for mobilization – for example, protest. But, when political arenas are sufficiently open and competitive, minority groups can mobilize through electoral channels, such as parties and elections. While protest and other forms of nonelectoral pressure may exert pressure on ruling majorities, the chief executive has the greatest incentive to secure the support of minority groups when they effectively mobilize in the electoral arena. Securing support can happen either publicly through coalitions or privately via backdoor channels. Additionally, if there is sufficient risk that a chief executive may lose power, incorporating minorities into the cabinet can be a strategic decision to appeal to voters from said group (Teele 2018; Valdini 2019). This is particularly prudent if the opposition has already incorporated minorities into their own ranks (e.g., Caul 2001; Weeks et al. 2023). While securing minority support can be initially achieved through rents, ultimately, the minority group will agitate for cabinet seats. A ministerial portfolio is what gives the group political prestige, access to more rents, and influence over politics – especially when compared to a legislative seat. The failure of the chief executive to include this group in the government can mean the difference between being in versus out of office.

The second mechanism is through **popular norms**: what the general population – especially those among the *double-hegemons* – believes. When there is a general expectation that the minority group should have a presence in the government, the chief executive cannot ignore the minority group or simply dole out rents. Instead, what matters is that the minority group is in the cabinet. While popular pressure can be independent of minority group size, these norms are more likely to manifest when minority groups are sizable. It may be easy to ignore a numerically small minority group, but the exclusion of a sizable group – either in proportional or absolute terms – is likely to generate reservations. Thus, failure to give minorities a seat at the table can mean a lack of political trust from the general population (at best) or removal from office (at worst). As a result of these two mechanisms, we see gender and/or ethnic minorities in cabinets.

Whether we see gender or ethnic minorities in the cabinet depends on whichever group offers the minimal winning coalition. Here, coalition is broadly defined. It is about a collection of actors whose joint cooperation (support) is necessary; the defection of one actor – that is, their withdrawal of political support – can undermine the likelihood of the others staying in power. Here, actors *can, but need not, be* a collection of parties in a parliamentary system that bargain over portfolios after elections (e.g., Germany). The collection of actors can also be elites agreeing to cooperate politically – whether it is within a party (e.g., the PAP in Singapore) or not (e.g., the military dictatorship in Taiwan). What matters here is whether minority groups are large enough and "useful to mobilize as bases of political support" (Posner 2005: 529).

Consequently, we see a zero-sum game between gender and ethnicity (Jensenius 2016; Karekurve-Ramachandra and Lee 2020). The political calculus changes, however, when (1) gender and ethnic groups are both politically competitive; and (2) there are popular norms regarding both groups being present in the government. At this point, we observe the following developments. One is that we see *double-minority* ministers. The presence of *double-minorities* in the cabinet proverbially kills two birds with one stone: it simultaneously addresses the competing demands of gender and ethnic minorities. And, under these conditions, research suggests that *double-minorities* may have a strategic electoral advantage: their multiple identities can appeal to a wider electorate (Bejarano 2013; Celis et al. 2014). Additionally, the presence of *double-minorities* in the cabinet recognizes the unique experiences of a distinct group: they are not just gender *and* ethnic minorities (additive) but rather ethnic minority women (multiplicative). For *double-minorities*, sexism and ethnic chauvinism interact in ways that are more than their mere summation (Crenshaw 1989; Davis 1983). In fact, accommodation on one identity dimension is not sufficient for ensuring accommodation on the other (e.g., Hughes 2011; Htun 2016). For example, when *double-minorities* fight for gender parity, they are often marginalized by other women because of ethnic differences. Conversely, when they advocate for ethnic inclusion, they are frequently sidelined by coethnic men.

As political competition increases, and as popular norms strengthen, the other observable development is that the presence of the coopted minority – whether singular or *double* – shifts away from tokenism. It is not just about having one or two minority ministers in the cabinet – where they oversee policy matters in their associated domain (e.g., women's affairs or cultural affairs). Once a minority group is in the government, it will continue to mobilize for more power, prestige, and policy influence. And it may do so against the backdrop of increasing public tolerance – if not outright popular support – for such efforts. As a result, we expect to see (more) minority ministers in portfolios of higher prestige that have far-reaching national implications (e.g., finance or foreign affairs).

In sum, we argue minority ministers – whether in terms of gender and/or ethnicity – gain more positions in cabinets when there is political competition or when there are popular norms for their inclusion. Importantly, competition and norms vary both across and within different regimes. Some democracies are more politically competitive than others, just as some autocracies are more socially tolerant than others. Moreover, given the conditional relationships between competition, norms, and minority group size, it is possible for autocracies to have diverse cabinets. For example, consider Singapore – and even Taiwan starting in the 1970s. Thus, our argument extends beyond a simple focus on regime types, and instead emphasizes the common mechanisms that explain when we see gender and/or ethnic minorities in cabinets across time and space.

1.1 Defining Minorities

Let us clarify what is – *and what is not* – a minority group. First, minority is **not a numerical-based definition**. Instead, we focus on the political powers and advantages held by the group. Thus, while women constitute at least 50% of the population, we consider them a gender minority because their political influence falls far short of that. Put differently, while men may constitute less than 50% of the population, they are a hegemon from a gender perspective. Likewise, we consider the ethnic group with the most political power to be the hegemon. Here, we follow Chandra (2006) and define ethnicity as an identity-based category in which membership is determined by descent-based attributes. The ethnic hegemon is often the largest ethnic group. However, this need not always be the case. In pre-2000 Taiwan, for example, a numerical minority politically oppressed the numerical majority (Wu 2021). Thus, the hegemon distinction is independent of whether the ethnic group is in fact a majority. It can be 90% of the population (e.g., Finns in Finland) or 40% of the population (e.g., Serbs in Yugoslavia). What matters is that these groups control the largest share of the political pie.

Second, minority is **not an ethnicity-only concept**. Since "minority" is about disproportional access to power, when we talk about minority ministers, minority portfolios, and minority presence in cabinets, it can be about gender or ethnicity – or both. And so, for clarification purposes, *double-minorities* are individuals politically underrepresented in both gender and ethnicity – that is, ethnic minority women. And conversely, *double-hegemons* are men from the hegemon ethnic group.

The focus on *double-minorities* is not important for just normative reasons. When it comes to singular identities, we know that descriptive representation has important consequences for substantive representation and equitable policy (Atchison 2015; Atchison and Down 2009; Betz et al. 2021; Reyes-Housholder 2016). We also know that descriptive representation matters for changing public attitudes (Barnes and Taylor-Robinson 2018; Morgan and Buice 2013). And while there is work suggesting the representation of intersectionality may function similarly (e.g., Annesley et al. 2015; Brown 2014; Hughes 2011; Paxton and Hughes 2015; Phillips 2021), we still lack broad comparative evidence on whether this is the case.

1.2 Cabinets versus Other Political Institutions

We focus on cabinets because doing so offers multiple empirical advantages. Cabinets – the group of political elites that counsel the chief executive and help them execute policies – exist in every country. They are not exclusive to democracies. Monarchs – for example, Hassanal Bolkiah of Brunei – have advisers; as do military officers – for example, Kenan Evren of Turkey. Even the most authoritarian and personalist dictatorships – for example, Albania under Enver Hoxha – have cabinets. Unlike legislative assemblies, judiciaries, or political parties, cabinets are the one institution that exists across regime types. If we are interested in minorities in governments, we risk a major selection bias if we focus only on institutions that exist primarily (and not randomly) in democracies. For example, a chief executive that can bar the existence of a legislature is likely to be unconstrained when it comes to choosing who is in their cabinet. Yet, if we looked only at the legislature, this country (e.g., Myanmar *1962–1974*) would be dropped from the sample.

Additionally, barring a few exceptions, cabinet ministers are not elected to their portfolios. Conversely, individuals are elected to legislative seats; likewise, individual parties win legislative elections. The public, however, does not vote on who should be the next agricultural minister. This feature gives us empirical leverage. When studying legislatures, we cannot easily disentangle why minorities are underrepresented. It could be because (1) minorities are barred from running; (2) voters are grossly chauvinist; or (3) parties are strategically putting up minority candidates in races where they simply cannot win. Since cabinet ministers are not elected, we can generally sidestep these selection biases.

This is not to say there are no selection biases with cabinet studies. We contend, however, that we can still theoretically account for these biases. For example, in some countries, there are rules that cabinet members must be drawn from the population of elected legislative members. What this means is that in an ethnically diverse country, if for whatever reason the legislature is composed exclusively of *double-hegemons*, the chief executive can only draw from this nondiverse pool. Regardless of why there are no gender or ethnic minorities in the legislature, the fact remains that neither minority group can constrain the chief executive. Put differently, they are politically noncompetitive and/or popular norms surrounding minority representation are weak. Another selection bias can manifest when it comes to coalition formation. Certain parties may champion a minority agenda – and therefore be composed of legislators from the minority group. Examples could include ethnic minority parties, which may not always win a lot of votes from the general electorate but do regularly win some proportion of votes from minority constituents. Another example could be a party that has adopted gender quotas (e.g., Green Parties; Wang, Fell and Peng 2023). If the party does well at the ballot box, it would follow that there are women legislators representing the party. In these cases, as formateurs build coalitions, these other parties will demand their members – that is, minorities – be included in the cabinet. In these cases, we see political competition and popular norms precisely at work. On the one hand, failure to give these politically competitive parties portfolios can mean the failure to form the coalition. On the other hand, including parties in the coalition when popular norms are vehemently opposed to them can also mean the government's downfall.

Finally, we focus on cabinets for a normative reason. Minority representation is important – not just in democracies but in authoritarian regimes as well. We know this from legislative studies. Yet, as we have established, the legislature is not a universal institution. Moreover, it is not the only high-profile institution. Arguably, the cabinet is just as high profile. If we care about how the presence of minorities matters for how the general population sees the government, it is imperative that we direct our attention to other institutions.

1.3 Putting Asia and Europe in Comparative Perspective with New Data

We focus on Asia and Europe for three reasons. The first is about Asia. On the one hand, there is an abundance of scholarship on representation in Asian countries – whether it is about gender in the Philippines (Cruz and Tolentino 2024) or South Korea (Kweon and Ryan 2022); ethnicity in Myanmar (Jap 2024) and Lebanon (Corstange 2013); or both gender and ethnicity in India (Brulé 2020; Varshney 2003) and Indonesia (Shair-Rosenfield 2019; Toha 2022). On the other hand, these works are almost always single-country studies. Absent is any comparative attention to larger trends and patterns across Asia (inclusive of the Pacific Basin) as an entire continent. This absence is concerning. Asia comprises 30% of the world's landmass and over 60% of the world's population. Across time and space, Asia encompasses *every political regime type* – from the totalitarian, personalist dictatorship of North Korea to the military regime of Thailand, from the party state of Laos to the liberal democracy of Mongolia. Asia is also a socially diverse region – whether it is about phenotype, language, or religion (see Liu and Ricks 2022; Selway 2015a). Empirically ignoring this important region limits our theoretical understanding of institutions, diversity, and politics.

But any inferences we draw about Asia – a region that we noted is heavily understudied – will inevitably raise questions of external validity. This brings us to our second reason. In contrast to Asia, Europe – especially the consolidated democracies of Europe – dominates the representation literature. Putting the two continents in direct dialogue will allow us to identify whether the observed patterns are specific to one region. It is also possible that comparing Europe to Asia will highlight the limits of the European cases with respect to external validity.

Third, and perhaps most importantly, putting the two regions in conversation with one another provides essential variation. We empirically explore our theory across ninety-three countries in Asia and Europe – spanning from Fiji and New Zealand in the east to Iceland and the United Kingdom in the west. Our temporal focus starts in 1960 – a data-imposed constraint – and ends in 2015. This spatial and temporal focus allows us to push the analysis across regime types. Just as democracies differ in their electoral rules and ideological composition, we see variation in authoritarian regimes (Gandhi 2008; Lee 2016). Institutionally, there are dictatorships governed by a party (e.g., the Hungarian Socialist Workers' Party), dictatorships controlled by a military (e.g., Spain under Francisco Franco), and dictatorships that are synonymous with an individual (e.g., North Korea's Kim Jong-Il *1994–2011*).

This empirical focus also brings variation in diversity. We compare ethnically diverse countries – for example, Afghanistan and the Netherlands – to some of the most ethnically homogenous ones – for example, Japan and Norway. But the diversity is not just at the societal level; it is also at the cabinet level. We compare the Soviet Union to China. These are two cases where women are consistently absent in the cabinets, but they are also two cases with strikingly different patterns with respect to ethnic minorities. Soviet cabinets were among the most ethnically diverse in the world, while Chinese cabinets have been filled almost entirely by ethnic hegemons. Contrast these two cases with the United Kingdom, which has had more gender-equitable cabinets, and India, which ranks relatively well when it comes to the presence of *double-minorities*. In short, focusing on Asia and Europe allows us to compare (1) homogeneous countries with cabinets dominated by *double-hegemons* at one extreme; (2) heterogeneous countries with diverse, intersectional cabinets at the other extreme; and (3) all the cases in between.

To build this data, we identified the gender and ethnicity of more than 32,000 unique ministers – for a total of almost 91,000 *country-year-minister* observations. Moreover, we create new measures that capture which minorities are in which portfolios by: (1) identifying an order based on objective rank; and (2) modifying an existing index based on subjective tiers (*Gender Power Score*; Krook and O'Brien 2012). Accordingly, the data not only identify when and where we see gender, ethnic, and *double-minorities* but also the prestige of their portfolios. Table 1 shows the top ten portfolios held by *double-minorities* in our dataset.

It is hard not to notice that many of these portfolios are associated with what Escobar-Lemmon and Taylor-Robinson (2005) classify as "low prestige" and/or with what Krook and O'Brien (2012) consider as "feminine." This is not to denigrate these portfolios. On the contrary, if the Minister of Women's Affairs or the Minister of Minority Affairs were a *double-hegemon*, this would raise

Table 1 Double-Minorities and Their Top Ten Portfolios

1.	Social Affairs	N=77
2.	Health	N=60
3.	Development	N=59
	Education	N=59
5.	Justice	N=50
6.	Youth	N=36
7.	Finance	N=31
	Foreign Affairs	N=31
9.	Environment	N=30
10.	Labor	N=29

questions and skepticism – if not outright anger and protest. And while these ministries may be necessary for minority representation, our contention is that they are not sufficient. Other ministries are responsible for policies with implications for gender and ethnic minorities, which a Minister of Women's Affairs or Minister of Minority Affairs might not be able to implement independently. These can include allowing women or transgender individuals in certain military units (Ministry of Defense); building paved roads into ethnic minority-concentrated areas (Ministry of Transportation); or enacting quotas for hiring practices (Ministry of Labor), university admission (Ministry of Education), and bank loans (Ministry of Finance). In this monograph, we are interested not only in whether there are *double-minorities* in the cabinet but also in their positions within the cabinet.

1.4 Monograph Layout

In Section 2, we review the scholarship on descriptive representation, noting the literature's general tendency to focus theoretically on one identity dimension and empirically on democracies. We then review some of the more important works addressing how intersectionality matters for political participation and representation (Brown 2014; Hughes 2011; Paxton and Hughes 2015; Phillips 2021; Tolley 2022). We contribute to (1) the ongoing conceptual call to appreciate the crosscutting nature of identities – that is, *double-minority* is not a residual category; (2) a theoretical framework for understanding the relationship between gender and ethnicity; and (3) the empirical attention to representation across regime types.

In Section 3, we look at the large-N statistical data. We discuss the coding scheme and offer some descriptive statistics. We then examine whether we see more gender and/or ethnic minorities in cabinets when there is more political competition from minority groups and when there are popular norms surrounding their presence in the government. After establishing *whether* these cabinets are indeed more diverse, we then test for (1) *which* minority groups are more likely to be present in the cabinet; and (2) *whether* political competition or popular norms matter more. We find that politically competitive countries with supportive popular norms and large ethnic minority populations are more likely than their less competitive and less supportive counterparts to have *double-minorities*. It seems both political competition and popular norms matter for cabinet composition, although the evidence suggests the latter has a larger effect.

Section 4 examines the significance of the minority presence – that is, whether it is tokenish. Not all ministries are equal in prestige. We discuss the two coding schemes for identifying portfolio ranks and test whether political competition and supportive popular norms result in minorities having more prestigious portfolios. We find that (1) while countries with supportive norms and with large ethnic minority populations do better than their counterparts, (2) the overall effects are still quite small – especially for *double-minorities*. The limited associations between political competition and popular support and the prestige of *double-minority* portfolios is in stark contrast to the stronger associations we find between these factors and *double-minority* descriptive presence. This discrepancy suggests a notable gap between the descriptive and substantive representation of intersectionality. Additionally, these results run counter to those where gender and ethnicity are considered singularly. While we find descriptive representation does lead to substantive representation (see Atchison 2015; Atchison and Down 2009; Betz et al. 2021; c.f., Kerevel 2019), we are reserved as to how much.

To give context to these large-N statistical tests, Section 5 offers a controlled comparison of four cases to illustrate how political competition from minority groups and popular norms for inclusion from the general public can influence cabinet composition. Specifically, we leverage the variation between **China** (monopoly of *double-hegemon* ministers), **the United Kingdom** (initial presence of white women in the cabinet and subsequent presence of *double-minority* ministers), **the Soviet Union/Russia** (presence of non-Russian men in the cabinet), and **India** (presence of different minorities, including *double-minority* ministers).

This analysis raises a question about democracy. On the one hand, we can think of democracy as a composite proxy for both political competition and popular norms. Consider that widely used democracy indices (e.g., *Varieties* of *Democracy* and *Polity*) are likely to code a country as a democracy if there are regularized elections and social liberalism. On the other hand, we can conceptualize democracy as something distinct from political competition and popular norms. Section 6 examines this question. The empirical results suggest that while democracy has a positive effect on cabinet composition, this effect is very much driven by political competition and popular norms. Once we control for both, the significant and positive effects disappear. We conclude by discussing future avenues of research – conceptually, theoretically, and empirically.

2 A Theory on Minorities in Cabinets

Descriptive representation is important. Yet, both gender and ethnic minorities have been historically marginalized, and this marginalization multiplies when gender and ethnicity intersect (Combahee River Collective 2014 [1977]; Crenshaw 1989). Gender-only minorities, ethnicity-only minorities, and *double-minorities* have long been denied a chance to exercise their voice and shape legislation. For example, in the first post-World War II decade, almost 88% of all cabinet ministers across Asia and Europe were men from their respective ethnic hegemon group. We are, however, seeing a shift toward more diverse cabinets. As Figure 3 shows, while these *double-hegemons* still occupy the vast majority of cabinet portfolios, there is also an increasing presence of minority ministers – both gender and/or ethnicity. **What explains this pattern?**

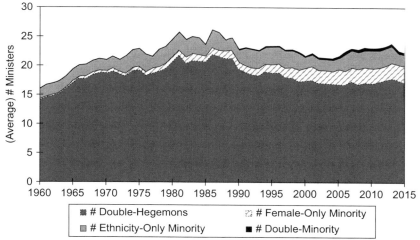

Figure 3 Number of Ministers per Group versus Average Cabinet Size by Year

2.1 Descriptive Representation in the Literature

There are two explanations for this trend. The first is an institutional one. Political systems alter the calculus of chief executives by influencing who gets elected and at what rate. Proportional electoral rules lead to higher levels of representation for women (McAllister and Studlar 2002; Paxton et al. 2010; Tremblay 2007). Proportionality may reduce the gender turnout gap (Teele 2023) and shift attention from candidates to parties (Krook and Schwindt-Bayer 2013) – leading to the political success of women. Moreover, higher district magnitudes reduce zero-sum competition – that is, when *either* a man *or* a woman gets elected – as candidates compete for multiple seats (Norris 2006; Trounstine and Valdini 2008). Existing work also identifies electoral gender quotas as a major determinant of women's political presence. Both cross- (e.g., Paxton et al. 2010; Paxton and Hughes 2015) and sub-national analyses (e.g., Barnes and Holman 2020; Burnet 2011) suggest that quotas change the way that parties recruit and nominate candidates with downstream consequences on whether electorates support women running for office.

The evidence linking electoral rules to ethnic minority representation is more mixed. Some contend that majoritarian (plurality) electoral rules are more likely to keep out minorities – even when they are sizable (Guinier 1994). Conversely, proportional electoral rules are supposedly more forgiving in allowing minority parties to secure legislative seats. This, in turn, affects the coalition bargaining game (Laver and Shepsle 1996). One interpretation is that such arrangements give minority parties a voice to demand portfolios (Lijphart 1999). Another interpretation, however, is that as minority parties seek to protect their group interests, they become veto players causing gridlock (Liu 2011; Selway 2015b). Yet, some studies suggest that, given the right contextual factors, ethnic minority candidates may be more successful in plurality systems. Moser (2008) finds the positive relationship between proportionality and ethnic minority representation is contingent on the presence of ethnic minority parties (also see Moser and Scheiner 2012). Finally, an emerging body of work – one we contribute to – investigates the intersectional nature of representation. We discuss these works in detail below.

It is not, however, just about the rules over *how* people can vote but *who* can vote. Even expanding the electorate can increase diversity in leadership. O'Brien (2012) finds that in Britain the simple act of changing the rules for choosing party leadership and for electing legislative committee chairs has increased the number of women in positions of power. In short, government cabinets are more diverse when the political system encourages power-sharing.

The second explanation, in contrast, focuses on social norms. Minority groups are often socioeconomically marginalized. Frequently, this marginalization comes hand in hand with being ostracized from the political arena (Blumberg 1984; Foxworth, Liu, and Sokhey 2015). But as societies modernize, (1) these disadvantaged groups can restructure traditional hierarchies – that is, call for greater equality (Inglehart and Norris 2003); and (2) the general public can support – or at a minimum, tolerate – gender equality and multiculturalism (Inglehart 1997). This support manifests as the belief that governments should reflect their citizenry (Borrelli 2002; Preuhs 2005). In short, governments are more inclusive when the public supports diverse representation.

Political systems that encourage power-sharing and public support for diverse representation have downstream consequences for both (1) the electoral success of parties championing minority populations; and (2) the motivations underpinning ministerial selection. In democracies, both factors are relevant for cabinet diversity. First, high levels of political competition – that is, a free and open arena – can facilitate the electoral success of multiple parties. This can include ethnic minority parties. It can also include other ideologically motivated parties that have adopted party quotas – for example, Green Parties with gender quotas (Wang, Fell, and Peng 2023). Second, if these parties are electorally successful, they can be attractive coalition partners due to their ability to mobilize and maintain a loyal electorate (Ghergina and Jiglău 2016). Third, chief executives can incorporate minorities into coalitions to signal their inclusiveness to electorates – but only if inclusivity is expected within the general population (Birnir and Satana 2013). Accordingly, if popular norms for inclusion are high, chief executives are more likely to incorporate minorities in cabinets. In sum, permissive electoral systems can lead to the electoral success of parties championing a minority group, these parties are attractive coalition partners, and popular norms can spur the selection of minorities as ministers. Thus, we see more diverse cabinets.

Autocracies, by definition, are less permissive than democracies. We do not expect the electoral success of parties championing a minority group to be as relevant for cabinet diversity simply because these parties are inherently less competitive in autocratic political arenas (e.g., Bernauer and Boschler 2011). This is not to say such parties are irrelevant (Liu, Gandhi, and Bell 2018). Even autocrats are responsive to public pressure, and parties or groups organized along ethnic lines can exert such pressure. We see this in Malaysia, for example, with the Malaysian Chinese Association and the Malaysian Indian Congress. Both parties have been important as evidenced by their inclusion in cabinets and in the recognition of their respective languages (Liu and Ricks 2022). Thus, if there are strong popular norms for diversity and inclusion, it can spur autocratic chief executives to select ethnic minority ministers.

We contend that previous work is limited in multiple ways. First, from a **conceptual** standpoint, the emphasis is frequently on one dimension of identity – for example, gender *or* ethnicity. Much of the literature characterizes the two identities as in an inherent competition when it comes to political representation (e.g., Arriola and Johnson 2014; Pierskalla et al. 2021). For example, focusing on subnational elections in India, Jensenius (2016) shows that women are more likely to be nominated for office in districts that have reserved seats for scheduled castes as opposed to other constituencies (also see Karekurve-Ramachandra and Lee 2020). Moreover, even if gender and ethnic minorities do not directly vie for access to office, the substantive representation of one group can limit that of the other (Htun 2016; Htun and Ossa 2013).

Yet, these identities do not always have to be in tension (Collins and Bilge 2016; Hughes 2011); instead, they can intersect. One literature investigates whether intersectional identities afford candidates an electoral advantage (see Mügge and Erzeel 2016). In certain contexts – for example, the case of Latinas in the United States (Bejarano 2013) – ethnic minority women tend to run for office and win to a greater extent than ethnic minority men. In these cases, multiple intersecting identities can lead to less discrimination – in both candidate selection and electoral support (Celis and Erzeel 2017; Celis et al. 2014; Hughes 2016). Yet, this "complementarity advantage" is context dependent. For example, focusing on local elections in Belgium, Janssen et al. (2021) find that left-leaning parties nominate minority men more than minority women in ethnically diverse districts. Other work directly challenges the electoral advantage of intersectionality, showing that minority women are systematically disadvantaged at every stage – from recruitment to selection – relative to both ethnic majority men and women (Tolley 2023). And, even when minority women compete for and win office, there are questions about whether they truly represent intersectional interests or if they were chosen by party leaders because they represent the interests of the dominant group (Murray 2016).

We build on this work by shifting the institutional focus to the cabinet. To the best of our knowledge, this is the first monograph looking at both gender and ethnicity simultaneously in cabinets. Yet, we build on a rich tradition of intersectional research that goes back to Kimberlé Crenshaw and other Black and multiracial feminists such as Frances Beal, Angela Davis, and Deborah King (see Hancock 2016). These works challenged race and gender as mutually exclusive categories and argued the problematic consequences for legal and policy outcomes (Crenshaw 1989). Moreover, ignoring intersectionality replicates and compounds inequities (Combahee River Collective 2014 [1977]; Crenshaw 1991). Thus, an intersectional analysis is not only reflective of lived realities (Anthias and Yuval-Davis 1983; Hughes and Dubrow 2018;

Lorde 1984; Smooth 2006) but also necessary to remedy the multiple systems of oppression faced by ethnic minority women (Collins 2000: 253; Davis 1983).

Second, from a **theoretical** standpoint, there is the assumption that all cabinet portfolios are functionally equivalent. Yet, this is not the case. Cabinets vary in their prestige and influence. Finance and foreign affairs, for example, are two of the more prestigious ministries in any country (Barnes and Taylor-Robinson 2018). Conversely, education (Apfeld and Liu 2021) and health (Selway 2015a) portfolios lack the same shine. Likewise, defense ministers tend to be men (Barnes and O'Brien 2018), while women's affairs ministers are almost always women (Krook and O'Brien 2012). This suggests not all portfolios are the same. We offer a theoretical explanation for not just *whether* there are minorities present in the cabinet but *where* in the cabinet.

The third limitation is an **empirical** one. The literature on cabinets has been long dominated by Western democracies – whether it is single-case studies, from the United States (Borrelli 2002) to Australia (Moon and Fountain 1997) to Canada (Studlar and Moncrief 1999) or cross-national large-N analyses (Escobar-Lemmon and Taylor-Robinson 2005; Krook and O'Brien 2008, 2012; c.f., Arriola and Johnson 2014; Barnes and O'Brien 2018). Likewise, works that focus explicitly on intersectionality are also largely limited to democracies (Bejarano 2013; Celis and Erzeel 2017; Janssen et al. 2017). Authoritarian regimes may lack regularized, multiparty elections. This does not mean, however, that they are devoid of political institutions for accommodating minority voices (Dowding and Dumont 2014; Gandhi 2008; Geddes, Wright, and Franz 2014; Meng 2020). Likewise, while dictatorships may be associated with more repression and curtailed freedoms, this does not preclude autocrats from espousing gender-egalitarian and/or multiethnic ideologies. In short, all leaders – regardless of regime – must appease their inner circle and public audience to varying extents (Kim and Gandhi 2010).

In this monograph, we address these limitations. First, we simultaneously consider both gender *and* ethnicity – noting that the two identities crosscut (Crenshaw 1989; Selway 2015a). We identify the circumstances when the two identities compete against each other. However, we also identify when it is no longer a zero-sum game: when the number of *double-minorities* increases, we empirically observe gender and ethnicity moving in tandem.

Second, we relax the assumption that all cabinet portfolios are of equal prestige. We employ two different measures to tap at these ranks: one is an objective ordered rank (Apfeld and Liu 2021); the other uses subjective categorical tiers (Escobar-Lemmon and Taylor-Robinson 2005; Krook and O'Brien 2012). And in doing so, we can differentiate between cabinets that: (1) have minorities in portfolios associated with their group identity (e.g., women's affairs for gender minorities or minority affairs for ethnic minorities) and (2) those that have minorities in more prestigious positions.

Third, we offer a generalized theory that travels across regime types. We begin with the premise that *double-hegemons* would prefer to concentrate political power among themselves. When this is not politically feasible, they must co-opt a minority group by bringing them into a government coalition. Initially, there is a trade-off between gender and ethnic minorities – that is, *double-hegemons* co-opt only one of the two. However, beyond a certain threshold – that is, when the political arena is sufficiently competitive *and* there is strong popular support for inclusion of both groups, we see the presence of *double-minorities* in the cabinet.

2.2 Our Argument

Individuals are an aggregation of multiple intersecting identities. While identity markers such as language, religion, and phenotype can vary in how much they overlap and crosscut – and they often overlap with geography (Liu and Selway 2024) and socioeconomic status (Selway 2007) as well – gender is different. Gender bifurcates (almost) every other identity group. Thus, when we focus on the intersection of gender and ethnicity, we are in fact operating in a scenario with *four* groups: (1) men from the ethnic hegemon group – that is, the *double-hegemon*; (2) women from the ethnic hegemon group – that is, the *gender-only minority*; (3) men from the ethnic minority group – that is, the *ethnicity-only minority*; and (4) women from the ethnic minority group – that is, the *double-minority*. Table 2 shows the relationship between these four groups.

Note that while we focus on gender and ethnicity, these are not the only two identities of sociopolitical relevance. A third cleavage can (1) bifurcate an otherwise homogeneous group or (2) homogenize an otherwise diverse set of groups. Given that individuals are an aggregation of multiple – if not an infinite number of – identities, we have made the explicit choice to focus only on the intersection of two. Doing so allows us to gain theoretical and empirical traction.

Table 2 Gender versus Ethnicity: The Four Groups

	Gender: Hegemon	**Gender: Minority**
Ethnicity: Hegemon	*Double-Hegemon*	*Gender-Only Minority*
Ethnicity: Minority	*Ethnicity-Only Minority*	*Double-Minority*

Our theory begins with the *double-hegemon* dominating the political landscape. When putting a cabinet together, the chief executive – very frequently a *double-hegemon* – has a finite number of portfolios to distribute. All else being equal, he prefers to allocate portfolios to fellow *double-hegemons* (Stockemer and Sundstrom 2019). There are two motivations. First, members from the same group tend to value the same things (Bates 1973; Miguel 2004). Second, members from the same group are more likely to have a common language. This shared vocabulary allows for efficiency in what would amount to repeated, regularized interactions (Csata et al. 2023; Habyarimana et al. 2009). Given this ingroup favoritism (and related outgroup disdain), we are likely to see *double-hegemons* populating the cabinet.

The ability of *double-hegemons* to monopolize the portfolios depends on whether they are *constrained* by a minority group – that is, whether the chief executive must *co-opt* some other group into his coalition to stay in power. If yes, this co-optation manifests as minority presence in the cabinet. For the potential ministers from the respective minority group, these portfolios are attractive: they offer access to political influence, they come with financial resources, and they are opportunities to engage in meaningful policy-making (Arriola and Johnson 2014; Ferree 2006).

Note that while the chief executive is frequently a *double-hegemon*, empirically there are exceptions – from Angela Merkel in Germany to Tsai Ing-wen in Taiwan. These are instances when the *double-hegemons* cannot hold on to all the portfolios; instead, they must co-opt a minority group. But the co-optation is not simply about one or two portfolios; instead, it requires something of great significance – that is, *the most* coveted portfolio. When the chief executive is not a *double-hegemon*, it is likely that they will champion for more minorities in the cabinet – for the same reasons a *double-hegemon* chief executive wants all *double-hegemons* in his cabinet. But again, how many minorities a minority chief executive can put in their cabinet will be constrained by the *double-hegemons* – that is, those who do hold the most political power.

The presence of minority groups in cabinets arises through two distinct – although not necessarily mutually exclusive – mechanisms. One is **political competition**. Given the threat of losing office, the chief executive can make a strategic calculation to have minorities in the cabinet. The competitive threat arises when a minority group is sizable and can mobilize. This mobilization can manifest through electoral channels such as voting or running for office. Consider how a minority party can voice demands for its demographic group and rally its constituents to vote. If this party is electorally successful, it sends a signal of the group's competitiveness. Political competition can also happen through nonelectoral means, such as protests – from sit-ins to blockades to riots.

While both mobilization pathways can exert pressure on the chief executive, we contend that the incentive to include minorities increases as political arenas become more open and competitive. In other words, increasing levels of *electoral competition* – that is, when minority groups formally organize and compete for office – lead to the greatest pressure on the chief executive. Failure of the chief executive to acknowledge the demands of the minority group risks removal. Additionally, the presence of minorities in the opposition can also incentivize the chief executive to include minorities. Here, the chief executive does not want *double-hegemon* rivals to gain an advantage. Thus, minorities in the government cabinet result from a strategic decision to forestall or minimize the potential gains of an opposition that has itself made the decision to include minorities.

Note that some demographic mass is *necessary* for representation. A group cannot functionally be present if it does not have some requisite demographic numbers. If there are no Wookies in the population, theoretically there can be no Wookies in the cabinet. Of course, whether a group exists is subject to politicization. On the one hand, governments can (try to) erase a minority group through repressive measures and/or by denying their existence on paper – for example, the Catalans in Spain (Bourne 2014; Woolard 1989) or the Romas in Romania (Csata, Hlatky, and Liu 2021; Csepeli and Simon 2004). On the other hand, governments can (try to) redraw the boundaries of the largest group by redefining the criteria for said markers – for example, the French (Weber 1976), the Greeks (Beaton 2020; Mylonas 2013), and the Yugoslavs (Ramet 2006).

At the same time, however, a large demographic mass is *not sufficient* for representation. Political institutions – from plurality electoral rules to gerrymandering to voting restrictions – can weaken an otherwise large minority group's voice (Minta 2011). For example, when a minority is geographically dispersed, even if they are sizable, their political voice is diluted (Jenne, Saideman, and Lowe 2007; Kasara 2007; Toft 2003; Weidmann 2009). In spite of the headcount, they cannot field candidates and have their votes aggregated in a meaningful way (Bernauer and Boschler 2011; Dancygier 2017). This is one common explanation for the underrepresentation of women despite their aggregate size: while women can be found in *all* districts, they are not concentrated in *any* district.

A minority group can also extract ministerial portfolios via **popular norms** – that is, when there is general support for their inclusion. Members of the minority group are not the only actors who can demand minority representation. Instead, the average citizen – most likely to be a *double-hegemon* – can also agitate. For example, there are men who identify as feminists and who believe in gender equity. Likewise, there are White Americans who acknowledge White privilege and support efforts to address structural racism. When there is a large ally population among the *double-hegemons*, this can constrain the chief executive to diversify the cabinet – knowing that doing so can offer an electoral advantage, and vice versa.

As societies modernize, ally populations grow. Members from minority groups that were once marginalized are better positioned to challenge the status quo. When they break these glass ceilings, they demonstrate that they deserve the same privileges afforded to *double-hegemons*. Moreover, emerging opportunities for intergroup contact facilitate understanding, promote position-taking, and inculcate tolerance among the general population. These repeated, regularized interactions translate into values of equity and inclusion – values supported (or at a minimum, tolerated) in government. In short, popular norms for diversity – while *not necessary* – are *sufficient* for minority inclusion in governments.

As evidence, consider the inverse – that is, what happens when public opinion among *double-hegemons* is staunchly opposed to minority inclusion? Here, weak public support can undermine an otherwise large minority group. For example, while women constitute roughly half of the population, widespread beliefs that "men make better political leaders than women do" (see Liu et al. 2017) mean women are often underrepresented (Reingold 2008). We see this gender gap manifesting with women being less politically knowledgeable and engaged than men (Liu and Banaszak 2017; Schuler 2019). Even within political institutions, these biases manifest: women are often formally denied the opportunities to hold positions of power (Preuhs 2006) and/or informally silenced, stereotyped, and rendered invisible (Hawkesworth 2003).

In sum, we are more likely to see minority ministers in cabinets when (1) there is political competition from a minority group and (2) there are popular norms for minority inclusion among the *double-hegemons*. Failure by the chief executive to give minorities a seat at the table can mean a lack of political trust. Theoretically, we are agnostic as to which of the two mechanisms matters more for cabinet composition – that is, *whether* there are minorities. We do contend, however, that when both mechanisms are present, we should see even more minorities – that is, *how many* minorities there are. In short, both mechanisms are *jointly necessary and sufficient* for high levels of minority presence in cabinets. The following hypotheses summarize this discussion:

Hypothesis 1.1: *We see more minorities in cabinets when minority groups are politically competitive.*

Hypothesis 1.2: *We see more minorities in cabinets when there are popular norms in favor of inclusion – particularly among double-hegemons.*

Importantly, political competition and popular norms vary both across and within regime types, and their effects may be conditional on group size. As women are generally 50% of the population, when we talk about **minority group size**, the focus is ethnic minorities. For example, consider Lebanon versus Greece. On the eve of independence, Lebanon's Christians were politically advantaged thanks to (1) a French colonial legacy and (2) a slim demographic majority per the 1932 Census (53%). However, the Sunni and Shia Muslims combined comprised over 40% of the population; and another religious group, the Druze, made up an additional 5%. In short, the Christians could not rule alone. The subsequent National Pact ensured that Maronite Christians would maintain control of the presidency – the most powerful political position – but also guaranteed top state positions to other religious communities (Hakim 2019). The first cabinet reflects this compromise: In addition to a Sunni Muslim prime minister, the defense minister was a Druze leader, and the minister of economy and trade and housing was a Shia politician.

In subsequent years, Lebanon's cabinet continued to be a site of contestation. A short civil war broke out in 1958 between the Lebanese government and a Muslim-Druze opposition, rooted in part by the latter's complaints of Christian dominance. As a compromise, political elites agreed to a "salvation cabinet," which for the first time contained an equal number of Christians and Muslims. The cabinet would also provide the coveted foreign affairs ministry to a Sunni Muslim (Sorby 2000).

In contrast to the Lebanese case, by the time Greece's right-wing junta crumbled (1974), top-down processes of Hellenization and conflict-driven demographic shifts had all but eliminated any ethnic minority groups. For example, estimates suggest the 1923 population exchange with Turkey removed as many as 400,000 Muslims from Greece (Motta 2013: 379). Likewise, Greece's Jewish population was decimated by the Holocaust. Whatever population remained was not large enough to require cooptation in a democratic Greece (Marrus 2011: 734). And then there were the Chams of Epirus – that is, Albanian-speaking Muslims; many fled or were expelled to Albania after collaborating with the Italian and German occupiers in World War II (Baltsiotis 2011).

Macedonian speakers numbered around 82,000 by the 1928 census (1.3% total population). Subjected to an aggressive Hellenization campaign under Ioannis Metaxas in the 1930s, the vast majority sided with the communists in Greece's civil war. After the communists' defeat, many Greek Macedonians retreated north (or were abducted) to Yugoslavia and the Soviet Union. Those who remained saw their position continue to deteriorate: the teaching of Macedonian was banned, Macedonians faced discrimination in hiring for civil service jobs, and Macedonian cultural performances were forbidden (Human Rights Watch 1994). For other ethnic minority groups, assimilation (Arvanites, Vlachs), marginalization (the Roma), or some combination of the two (Albanians after 1991) was so complete that they have never registered politically.

The only ethnic minority to achieve any kind of recognized political representation were the Muslims of Western Thrace. Officially protected by the Treaty of Lausanne and excluded from the population transfer in 1923, they currently number around 120,000. Constituting more than half the population in Rhodope province, and significant percentages in Xanthi and Evros, they leveraged this geographical concentration to secure two parliamentary seats (Nohlen and Stöver 2010). But this is the extent of national-level minority electoral success. With the Muslims constituting just 1% of the total population, it is not surprising that they have been absent from the cabinet. In sum, group size matters – not in and of itself but because of how it directly manifests through political competition. Specifically:

Corollary 1: *The association between the presence of minorities in cabinets and political competition increases as minority groups become larger in size.*

Importantly, even authoritarian regimes are responsive to political competition of minorities and/or popular support for minorities. For example, minority groups protest in authoritarian regimes. And in fact, it may even be in the autocrat's interest to allow minority groups to form parties and contest legislative elections. Doing so divides the opposition – particularly isolating out the more radical elements (Lust-Okar 2005) – and gives the autocrat some control within institutional channels for policy-making without appearing publicly weak (Gandhi 2008). Likewise, the general population in authoritarian regimes can also believe in gender and/or ethnic equality. We see this in communist regimes when governments espouse such ideologies. We also see this in countries facing "systemic vulnerability" (Doner, Ritchie, and Slater 2005) – that is, when governments face such structural threats that they are forced to make large concessions to everyone to calm domestic dissent.

Consider Jordan. Despite comprising a demographic majority, Jordanian citizens of Palestinian origin are politically marginalized relative to those of East Bank descent. Yet, at various points throughout Jordan's post-independence history, the country's leaders have awarded cabinet positions to Palestinian elites to secure the group's continued loyalty to the monarchy. For example, in 1970, King Hussein appointed a Jordanian of Palestinian descent, Abdel Monem Rifai, to serve as prime minister and form a "cabinet of reconciliation." The cabinet was to feature multiple Palestinian ministers and supporters of the Palestinian Liberation Organization (PLO) – which was then headquartered in Jordan. The appointment followed a series of violent clashes between government troops and PLO militants; it represented an effort by the king to mollify the PLO's sympathizers (Pace 1985). Similarly, in the early 1990s, as (1) Israeli–Palestinian negotiations began with the support of Amman and (2) King Hussein started negotiating a peace treaty with Israel – both of which were opposed by the majority of Palestinians in Jordan – Hussein granted the prestigious positions of foreign affairs minister and then prime minister to a Palestinian, Taher Masri. The move was widely interpreted as an attempt by the regime to deter potential Palestinian mobilization against its unpopular diplomatic ventures (Brand 1999; Brinkley 1991). The following corollary summarizes this discussion:

Corollary 2: *The association between the presence of minorities in cabinets and popular norms for minority representation increases as minority groups become larger in size.*

Thus far, we have remained theoretically agnostic over which minority identity – that is, gender or ethnicity – the chief executive co-opts. And anecdotally, this is the case. In Britain, the cabinet welcomed a woman many decades before it included a non-White minister. Conversely, in the Soviet Union, we see more – *a lot more* – ethnic minorities than gender minorities. We argue when the chief executive is constrained to co-opt, it will choose the minority group that yields the most political support for the fewest portfolio allocations – that is, the minimum winning coalition (see Posner 2005). Whichever group it chooses, this becomes the primary relevant identity around which politics is then subsequently organized.

While politics may mobilize around this one identity dimension, this does not preclude competition from minorities on the other dimension (Arriola and Johnson 2014). There is a limit in the number of cabinet portfolios. And while it is possible to expand cabinet size – which, as we saw in Figure 3, does empirically happen – there is still a zero-sum feel. In fact, it is in the interest of the recognized minority group to exclude other groups. Doing so maximizes said group's political prestige, access to rents, and influence over policies. Likewise, for the chief executive, the presence of a second minority group in the cabinet means fewer portfolios allocated *to double-hegemons*. And recall, the reason the chief executive co-opted one minority group in the first place was because it was the one that offered the minimum winning coalition. In short, once a minority group is recognized, there is a sense of institutionalized path-dependence – that is, there is a status quo bias.

These calculations, however, can change when minority groups on both dimensions become politically competitive and/or the general public believes in the inclusion of both groups. When this happens, we are likely to see two developments. The first is that the previously excluded minority group will mobilize and extract concessions. However, at some point, once the chief executive seeks to co-opt both minority groups, their demands multiply. Moreover, these demands may be orthogonal to one another – if not in direct conflict. Here, there is an incentive for the chief executive to include *double-minorities* in the cabinet. From an instrumental standpoint, the presence of *double-minorities* allows the government to proverbially kill two birds with one stone: to increase the presence of gender *and* ethnic minorities – at a point when it may not be possible to simply just increase cabinet size. Additionally, there is an identity-based reason to include *double-minorities* in the cabinet: They are a distinct minority group that is neither just gender nor ethnic minorities but an intersection of both. As such, their experiences are distinct and unique – and they too can mobilize as an electoral block and have allies. Specifically, we argue the following:

Hypothesis 2.1: *Politically competitive states have more double-minorities in their cabinets than politically uncompetitive states.*

Hypothesis 2.2: *States with popular norms in favor of inclusion have more double-minorities in their cabinets than states without popular norms in favor of inclusion.*

The second development is that the previously included minority group will agitate for more influence (e.g., Goddard 2019; Lee and Park 2018). There will be a demand for ministerial portfolios beyond the traditional ones associated with the minority group (e.g., women's affairs or minority affairs) – or even those that are somewhat neutral (e.g., tourism). Instead, there will be calls for minority ministers to assume the more prestigious posts (e.g., finance or foreign affairs) – and possibly even the appointment of one as a deputy prime minister. Given this discussion we argue that:

Hypothesis 3.1: *Politically competitive states have more minorities in prestigious positions than politically uncompetitive states.*

Hypothesis 3.2: *States with popular norms in favor of inclusion have more minorities in prestigious positions than states without popular norms in favor of inclusion.*

2.3 Discussion

In this section, we argued that politically competitive states and states with inclusionary popular norms – on average – (1) not only have more minority ministers in their cabinets, but they are (2) more likely to have *double-minorities* and (3) to have them in higher prestige portfolios. Minority groups – if they are sufficiently large enough – can be a threat to the chief executive either at the ballot-box or on the streets. Likewise, allies can exert pressure on leaders to be more inclusive. When the *double-hegemons* are okay with – or even advocate for – minority representation, this can affect the calculus of cabinet composition. In the next sections, we test our argument.

3 Minorities and Cabinet Compositions

Consider Yugoslavia. From 1960 to 1990 the country had multiple non-Serb ministers each year – constituting at least 60% and up to almost 90% of the cabinet. Given Yugoslavia's ethnic and political composition, this is not wholly surprising. Yugoslavia was comprised of six republics and two autonomous provinces (Kosovo and Vojvodina). These boundaries largely mapped to the country's six constituent nations. The need to balance competing interests was clear, and thus, cabinet positions were distributed accordingly. While there were no formal quotas, it was common practice to include two representatives from each republic and one from each autonomous province in executive leadership roles. And in a country where the largest ethnic group – Serbs – never made up more than 40% of the population,[1] it is noteworthy that they rarely held more than 40% of available cabinet seats.

As president, Josip Tito's first priority was national unity – that is, ethnic harmony. Consequently, women got the short end of the stick. While communist ideology and practice were relatively favorable to women's rights, when it came to cabinet composition, Yugoslavia's ethnic geopolitics took precedence. From 1960 to 1990, there were only four women in the cabinet. By comparison, in independent Serbia, women have routinely occupied more than 10% of available cabinet positions – with as much as 20% in recent years. In fact, Serbia's longest-serving prime minister, Ana Brnabić, is a lesbian.

This pattern in Yugoslavia-turned-Serbia is consistent with what we discussed in the previous section: We expect to see more minorities in government cabinets when one of two mechanisms is present. The first is that there is political competition. Failure to accommodate a large minority population could mean the difference between staying in office and being ousted. The second is that there

---

[1] Serbs only break the 40% threshold by counting Bosnian Serbs who – at the time – were understood as representing the interests of the Socialist Republic of Bosnia and Herzegovina.

are popular norms recognizing the value of minority inclusion. When minorities have the freedom of assembly, media, and speech, it can inculcate general awareness of their demands among the *double-hegemons* – thereby perpetuating some sort of public support. In this section, we test this argument.

3.1 Identifying Gender and Ethnicity of Cabinet Ministers

We employ a newly constructed dataset of all cabinet ministers across all Asian and European countries 1960–2015 – inclusive of the now defunct Yugoslavia and its successor states (e.g., Bosnia and Kosovo), those spanning the Asia-Europe divide (e.g., Armenia, Azerbaijan, and Georgia), and the island states (e.g., Australia, Cyprus, and Iceland). In all, we identify the gender and ethnicity of more than 32,000 unique ministers – for a total of almost 91,000 *country-year-minister* observations (which we subsequently collapse into N=4,049 *country-year* observations).

We begin by scraping the printed annual versions of the *Europa World Yearbook*. We do not use Bank's *Political Handbook of the World* or the CIA's *World Factbook* because these alternative sources list the cabinet ministers alphabetically in English per their ministry names. This is an important feature that will become relevant in Section 4 – and also the reason why our temporal analysis begins in 1960. But as is, for each *country-year*, we have a list of individuals and their respective ministries.

We employ a multi-stage strategy to identify the gender and ethnicity of each minister. In the first stage, we used student coders to read through the biographies of each minister in English – and if possible or necessary, the corresponding local language. Biographies included ministry websites, government documents, newspaper articles, and Wikipedia. We asked each student to identify any evidence that the minister was not a man from the ethnic hegemon group.

Note that it is always easier to find evidence that a minister is a gender minority than a gender hegemon. For example, biographical profiles are likely to mention someone as the "first woman" as opposed to the "*n-th* man." Other clues to suggest a minister's gender include family tree – for example, they are the mother, sister, wife, or daughter of *y*. It can also include their membership in some women's organizations. For an example, see Appendix 3A (Romania's Sulfina Barbu). Of course, this strategy risks rendering ministers with more gender-neutral accolades (e.g., no "first woman") or even gender-neutral names (e.g., Adraste or Aurèle) as men. It also denies transgender and nonbinary identities among those who do not publicly identify as such. Our hope is that these false negatives are far and few. However, for those who have such identities, our coding scheme would consider them as gender minorities.

Gender, Ethnicity, and Intersectionality in Cabinets 27

Likewise, it is relatively easy – although a little harder than gender – to identify ethnic minority ministers. Surnames often embed an ethnolinguistic marker. Other pieces of evidence include their *hometown*, their proficiency in the *minority language*, and their *political affiliation*. See Appendix 3B for an example (Romania's Zsolt Nagy). Admittedly, these markers are far from perfect. A minister could be multiethnic. But as a reminder, our focus here is *whether* a minister is an ethnic minority and not *which* ethnic minority. The bigger concern is a false negative – that is, coding an ethnic minority as an ethnic hegemon. However, since we can only code based on whatever information is publicly available – the same information available to the general public – it is our hope that these false negatives are the exceptions and not the norm.

The fact that *double-hegemons* are such a common occurrence in cabinets means there is relatively scant attention paid to either their gender or ethnicity. This is in stark contrast, for example, to the rhetoric surrounding Kamala Harris in the American context – first woman, first African American, and first Asian American and Pacific Islander. As another example, compare the Hillary Clinton versus John Kerry narratives – two former State Secretaries, Senators, and Presidential candidates. One could not be mentioned without referencing her gender; the other, no mention of his gender whatsoever. If there is no corroborating evidence of any sort, the student coded the minister as a *double-hegemon*.

We compare the coding for each minister across the multiple coders in the second stage. Note that each minister had at least three coders. We validated both internal consistency and external validity. Let us walk through an example. Former US Transportation Secretary Elaine Chao is a Chinese immigrant from Taiwan. In spite of the clear lineage, there is no "Chinese" ethnic group in either the *All Minorities at Risk* (Birnir et al. 2015) or *Ethnic Power Relations* (Cederman, Wimmer, and Min 2010) datasets. This is noteworthy as the two datasets employ different methods for categorizing ethnic groups: One uses government-reported documents (e.g., the census) and newspaper articles; the other, country expert surveys. Both datasets, however, identify "Asian" as a minority group. Moreover, one of the two classifies "Chinese" as a subgroup of "Asian". And so in this case, we code Chao as "Asian" – that is, an ethnic minority. It is possible that Chao does not self-identify broadly as Asian but rather specifically as Chinese/Taiwanese. Alternatively, it is possible that whether she identifies as Asian or Chinese is context-driven. But what matters here is not *which* minority group the minister identifies with, but *whether* they identify as one.

Let us consider another example: Chao's successor, Pete Buttigieg. Buttigieg is Maltese on his father's side. "Maltese" is not an ethnic group in either dataset.

Moreover, unlike Chinese, Maltese is not a subgroup of any relevant minority race or ethnicity. This suggests Maltese is not a socially relevant category in the US. In this case, we code Buttigieg as "non-Hispanic white" – a category that the general American public and likewise American race and ethnic politics scholars would see him as. In short, if a minister's ethnic identity appears in either one of the two lists (e.g., Hispanic in the US), we consider the minister an ethnic minority; if it does not (e.g., Swedes in the US), we consider the minister a member of the ethnic hegemon group.

With the updated list, we then crowd-sourced in the third and final stage for a subset of countries (see Sumner, Farris, and Holman 2020). For countries where we lacked the in-country familiarity, we created a list that included *all* identified ethnic minority ministers, *all* the ministers we had corrected back to the hegemon ethnic group, and a random sample of ministers from the hegemon ethnic group. We then crowd-sourced the verification of this list – a list with only the names and their ministries – with people from the country (target: two per country). We asked these individuals to identify whether the ministers are of the hegemon ethnic group or a member of a minority group. We then cross-checked their responses to what we have. There was general agreement in the coding. Where there was not, we deferred to local experts.[2]

3.2 Research Design

To measure cabinet composition, we collapse the dataset to the *country-year* unit of analysis. We see a large range in the number of portfolios across countries, from minimum of 1 (*Laos-1960*) and 2 (*Bhutan-1970*) to maximum of 79 (*Soviet Union-1973*) and 93 (*North Korea-1989*). The mean is 22.3. Note, however, that cabinet sizes are certainly not fixed. Thus, we focus on the proportion of portfolios held by the *double-hegemons* over time. Note that this is the raw data used to generate Figure 2.

On the right-hand side, we have two primary explanatory variables. The first is **political competition** – that is, the extent to which minority populations

---

[2] In multiple cases, ethnicity is defined not only by phenotype, language, and religion but also generation – that is, when the person's ancestors arrived in the country. Thus, two people may be of the same "ethnicity" to an outsider – for example, Chinese – yet they are considered to be of two different ethnicities by the locals. This was common in multiple Asian cases. For example, consider the "Chinese" in Cambodia, Myanmar, and Thailand. Ministers who could trace their lineage to China are considered members of the hegemon ethnic group because of the many generations that they have been in the country (Liu and Ricks 2022). The generation element is not simply about time; instead, it is about them having fully integrated into the local (hegemon) culture which includes knowing the language. Put differently, a new immigrant from China who can speak the local language would not be considered part of the ethnic hegemon group. A conceptual parallel in the US context would be a Black person who is a descendant of freed slaves versus a first-generation immigrant from Africa.

politically mobilize. Here, we use Bormann and Golder's (2013) measure of the *effective number of parties* (per vote share). The intuition is that when there are *k* political parties, this suggests there are *k-1* issue dimensions (Cox 1997; Laakso and Taagepera 1979; Taagepera and Grofman 1985). And when *k* is not small, it follows that these issue dimensions would include matters related to gender and/ or ethnicity. Examples of this include ethnic minority parties – from the Movement for Rights and Freedoms in Bulgaria to the Swedish People's Party of Finland to Balad in Israel. When these parties enter a government coalition, they can extract portfolios for ethnic minorities. Political competition, however, can also happen outside the confines of smaller parties and coalition politics. Large parties can jostle and compete for votes by advocating for particular issues – for example, women's rights and gender equity. In short, as the number of effective parties increases, we should see more salience of minority issues – manifesting in the presence of minority ministers in the cabinet.

The variable – in its original form – ranges from 1.78 (*Bangladesh-2014* and *Bangladesh-2015*) to 13.86 (*Poland-1991* and *Poland-1992*). Note, however, that the measure only exists for countries that are considered democracies – that is, only 56% of our sample. While authoritarian regimes are by definition non-democracies, some do govern with democratic-like institutions, for example, parties competing in legislative elections. And whether an authoritarian country allows for parties is certainly not random. Instead, it reflects a constrained dictatorship needing to co-opt an opposition (Gandhi 2008). In short, authoritarian regimes are diverse, and we must account for this variation. For the missing authoritarian *country-year* observations, we code them as a 1 if the country is considered a party dictatorship per Geddes, Wright, and Frantz (2014); otherwise a 0. With this coding scheme, about 43% of the authoritarian *country-year* observations are considered party dictatorships – that is, 19% of the full sample.[3]

The other explanatory variable of interest is **popular norms** – that is, what are the effects of having a large liberally inclined ally population that supports diversity. Here, we use data from the World Values Survey (WVS) – the largest cross-national survey (*N*=90) dating back to 1981. To measure gender parity, we look at a battery of questions (*N*=17) that ask respondents how much they agree with statements such as "Men make better politicians than women," "It is a problem if women have more income than men," and "Home and children is what most women really want."[4] Answers range anywhere from a three-point to

---

[3] The results are robust when we consider Freedom House's *political rights* (which only begins in 1973), Polity's *competitiveness of executive recruitment,* and Varieties of Democracy's *electoral democracy.*

[4] See Appendix 3C for the full list of seventeen questions used.

a five-point scale depending on the question. We normalize all responses to a 0 to 1 scale and take the average value across all questions. For ease of interpretation, we set 1 to represent the more gender-equitable attitude – that is, higher values suggest higher support for equality.

Next, to measure attitudes toward ethnic outgroups, we focus on the neighbor question: "Could you please mention any [from this list] that you would not like to have as neighbors?" The list is extensive, including drug addicts, homosexuals, and heavy drinkers. For our purposes, we focus only on those who mentioned "people of a different race" and/or "people who speak a different language." We use the neighbor question as opposed to the more general trust question (e.g., "Do you trust people of another nationality?") because it taps more at a desire – if not an outright behavior – as opposed to a disposition. Someone can be generally trusting, but not want an ethnic outgroup neighbor. Additionally, it is hard to ascertain whether respondents – when prompted to think of someone of another nationality – are thinking about someone of another nationality in their home country (e.g., the Chinese in the United States) versus people of that other nationality in general (e.g., the Chinese or the Chinese in China). Again, we normalize responses on a 0 to 1 scale and construct the variable such that 1 suggests no mention of – that is, tolerance – ethnic outgroups. We then multiply this measure with the one for gender equity to create an aggregate measure for popular norms.

We collapse the WVS data – from a *country-survey year-individual* unit of analysis – to a *country-year* unit of analysis. This yields a dataset with $N=182$. Note that this number is quite low for multiple reasons. First, while WVS is the largest cross-national survey, it does not include every country. Second, even if a country was included, it is possible that the requisite questions – about gender and/or ethnicity – were not asked. And third, while WVS began in 1981, it is not surveyed every year. To date, there have been only seven waves.

However, since norms do not change drastically from one year to the next, we interpolate the missing data between survey years. For example, Turkey is surveyed in 2001 and 2006. Here, we use a linear interpolation for the 2002–2005 missing years. In doing so, this gives us $N=779$ observations. Countries scoring the lowest on popular norms include Bangladesh (0.573 in 2002) and Jordan (0.687 in 2007). And at the other end, those scoring the highest include Sweden (0.997 in 2006) and Norway (0.996 in 2007).

Naturally, we are nervous resting our empirics strictly on such a small sample – especially considering it is a nonrandom sample (Kao, Liu, and Wu 2023). A simple means test suggests that countries included in WVS have on average 74.9% *double-hegemons* in their cabinets; in contrast, countries not included have on average 81.6%. Likewise, in terms of political competition, countries surveyed in WVS have 3.289 effective number of parties; those not surveyed, 2.353 – a statistically significant difference.

As an alternative, we conceptualize popular norms as democratic norms and measure it as *democratic stock*: countries that have more compound experience with democracy are more likely to have social norms valuing diversity (Gerring, Thacker, and Alfaro 2012). To measure democratic stock, we simply count the number of years a country has been a democracy (per Cheibub, Gandhi, and Vreeland 2010).[5] The mean for democratic stock is nine years – although the median is one. And note that the difference in democratic stock between countries included in WVS and those not included is 15.348 versus 7.847 – suggesting that if anything, by looking at the democratic stock for the full sample, we are biasing the results against us.

We also consider *ethnic minority group size*. The intuition is that there must be ethnic minorities in the general population for cabinets to have ethnic minorities.[6] Here, we use data from the *Ethnic Power Relations* dataset (Cederman et al. 2010). We identify ethnic hegemons as the ones with the highest ranking political status, whether it is a monopoly (1), a dominant group (2), or a senior partner (3). Instead of coding for the size of the hegemon ethnic group, we look at the inverse – that is, the total size of everyone else (*1-ethnic hegemon group size*). This allows us to directly measure how chief executives behave as the constraints they face increase. Note that ethnic minority group size ranges from 0 to 0.884. A high value could indicate either the political tyranny of a numerical minority (e.g., pre-2000 Taiwan) or the presence of multiple ethnic minority groups (e.g., India and Indonesia).

Across the decades, we see a mean minority population size of 26%. As a reminder, this 26% does not necessarily indicate one singular minority group. It does, however, suggest that the average size for the ethnic hegemon group is around 74% of the population. And in fact, in almost 5% of the *country-year* observations, the ethnic hegemon group is effectively the entire population – that is, minority group size is 0. At the same time, the ethnic hegemon group is not always the majority – if even the plurality. At the most extreme are the likes of Taiwan, where a numerical minority (Waishengren) repressed and then later co-opted the numerical majority (Benshengren).

For other covariates on the right-hand side, we also consider the wealth of country *i* in year *t*. Wealth matters since poverty "pressure[s] the upper strata to

---

[5] The results are robust when we consider Freedom House's *civil liberties* (which only begins in 1973), Polity's *competitiveness of participation*, and Varieties of Democracy's *liberal democracy*.

[6] We focus on ethnicity as opposed to gender since we see assume the proportion for women on average is constant spatially across countries and temporally over time – that is, approximately 0.50.

treat the lower classes as beyond the pale of human society," whereas in its absence, "tolerance norms" develop (Lipset 1959: 83–84). We use *GDP per capita* (source: UN Statistics). We also code for the *colonial legacy* given that the British were more likely to favor direct rule and multiculturalism in government institutions (La Porta et al. 1999). In all, we identify six colonial legacy types: American, Australian, British, Dutch, French, and none. We also consider regions. Countries that are contiguous are more likely to have shared histories in the same empire and thus hold similar cultural values in the contemporary – whether it is about gender equity or the position of ethnic minorities. We include dummies for seven regions: Western Europe, Eastern Europe (inclusive of post-Soviet Central Asia), West Asia (Middle East), South Asia, Southeast Asia, East Asia, and Pacific. The data source for both colonial legacy and region is Wahman et al. (2013).

Since cabinet compositions do not usually change drastically from one year to the next, we include a lagged dependent variable. We also consider country fixed effects given possible country-level confounders. And finally, we use decade fixed effects. This allows us to account for period-specific trends (e.g., the third wave of democratization). Moreover, we can account for general over-time trends such as increasing minority inclusion at all levels of government and increasing cabinet sizes.

3.3 Empirical Evidence

We first test for *whether* governments facing either political competition and/or popular norms have more minorities in their cabinets. We run a series of ordinary least squares (OLS) regressions, where the dependent variable is the proportion of *double-hegemons*. At this point, we are agnostic as to *which* minority groups are present in the cabinet. All we care about in **Hypothesis 1.1** and **Hypothesis 1.2** is *whether* certain countries have lower proportions of *double-hegemons*. Table 3 shows the regression results. As we see in the first model, the effects are significant and *negative* for the *effective number of parties*, suggesting governments facing political competition have smaller proportions of *double-hegemons* in the cabinet.

We see similar patterns when we shift to popular norms. Model 2 looks at public attitudes per WVS. As attitudes toward gender equity and tolerance of ethnic outgroups increase, the proportion of *double-hegemons* decreases. And the effect – up to a 6% contraction when shifting one standard deviation below the mean to one standard deviation above – is not trivial. This is the equivalent of a 20-person cabinet going from all *double-hegemons* to one with a minority minister. Note, however, the large drop in the number of observations. To

Table 3 Effects of Political Competition and Popular Norms on Portfolio Proportions for Double-Hegemons

	Political Competition	Popular Norms: Attitudes	Popular Norms: Stock
	(1)	(2)	(3)
Ethnic Minority Size	−0.077 (0.098)	0.156 (0.086)*	−0.069 (0.064)
Effective # Parties	−0.003 (0.001)†		
Attitudes: WVS		−0.252 (0.072)‡	
Stock: # Years Democracy			−0.001 (0.000)‡
Constant	0.394 (0.025)‡	−0.296 (0.077)‡	0.532 (0.077)‡
N	2910	677	2349
R²	0.90	0.92	0.89
Root MSE	0.06	0.06	0.06

Notes. Dependent variable: Proportion of cabinet held by *double-hegemons*. Results are from OLS regressions with GDP per capita, colonial dummy, region dummy, lagged dependent variable, country fixed effects, and decade fixed effects. Standard errors in parentheses. *p≤0.10; †p≤0.05; ‡p≤0.01

address this concern, we consider the number of years a country has been a democracy as an alternative measure for popular norms. We are cognizant that the democratic stock measure is at a very macro level. Undoubtedly, it is the inverse of the attitudes measure: while the WVS measure was much more precise, we were left with a large number of missing observations; conversely, while we now have a crude measure, missing data is no longer a concern. The hope is that if the results are similar between the two measures, it gives us some confidence in our inferences. And as Table 3 shows, the effects remain significant and negative.

Putting the three models together, we see that both constraints matter for cabinet composition. But on average, it seems that of the two, it is popular norms that have larger effects. We return to this later in this section. Next, having established *whether* governments are more likely to have minorities in their cabinets when faced with political competition and popular norms (answer: yes), we set out to identify *which* minority groups.

Here, we use a compositional model. Since the proportion of portfolio for all four groups must collectively add up to 1, it reasons that when the proportion for one group goes up, it must go down for at least one other group. We first convert the proportions into an unbounded scale with a multivariate logistic transformation. We then calculate the natural log of each minority type in reference to the *double-hegemon* proportion:

$$Y_{it} = \left[ln\left(\frac{Gender - Only\ Minority_{it}}{Double - Hegemon_{it}}\right), ln\left(\frac{Ethnicity - Only\ Minority_{it}}{Double - Hegemon_{it}}\right), ln\left(\frac{Double - Minority_{it}}{Double - Hegemon_{it}}\right) \right]$$

Finally, after transforming the dependent variables, we take the log ratios and model them with a seemingly unrelated regression (SUR) (Tomz, Tucker, and Wittenberg 2002; see Barnes, Beall, and Holman 2021). The results are substantively robust if we run the models separately (see Appendix 3D).

Recall, in **Hypothesis 2.1** and **Hypothesis 2.2**, we argued that governments accommodate more *double-minorities* when there is political competition and/or popular support. However, for there to be *double-minorities* there need to be ethnic minorities in the population in the first place. Consider a case where there is no sizable ethnic minority group, such as Greece or Japan. There is no reason to assume an ethnic minority will be included in the government – regardless of gender. In such cases, our expectations would be that if there were minorities in the cabinet, it would be gender-only minorities (as we assume women constitute 50% of the population in every country). This discussion highlights the importance of interacting political competition and popular norms with ethnic minority group size.

The SUR results (see Appendix 3E) show that when it comes to political competition, (1) the effect of ethnic minority size is not a statistically significant predictor for the proportion of hegemon women in the cabinet, but (2) it matters for whether we see more ethnic minorities in the cabinet – of either gender. Additionally, when we consider the conditional effects of political competition, we see a significant and positive effect on the proportion of *double-minorities* – and only for the *double-minorities*. This is all consistent with **Hypothesis 2.1.**

To grasp substantive impact, we plot marginal effects. In Figure 4, the top row focuses on the marginal effects when shifting from low political competition (*effective number of parties*=0) to high (*effective number of parties*=5.72). In the top left panel, when the ethnic minority group size is small (i.e., 2%), we see that as political competition increases, the average proportion of single-minorities increases as well. Note, however, the effects are neither statistically different from an effect of 0 nor different from each other. But what is significant – but in a negative direction – is that of *double-minorities*. This suggests that as competition increases, and when the ethnic minority population is small,

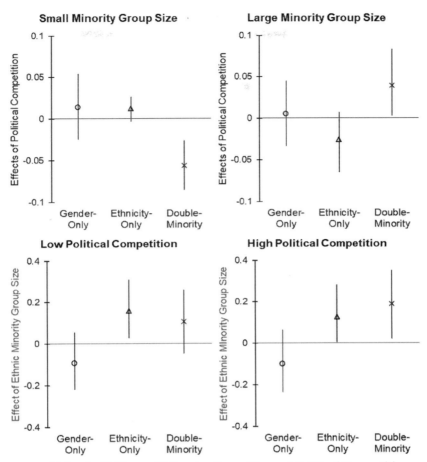

Figure 4 Marginal Effects of Minority Group Size and Political Competition on Cabinet Proportions

there is an inherent zero-sum dynamic between gender and ethnicity – coming at the expense of the *double-minorities*.

But what happens when the ethnic minority group size is large (e.g., 57.2%)? Several observations are worth noting. First, the effects for the gender-only minority are again not significant. And in fact, the effects mirror those from the first panel. Second, we see the importance – and relevance – of the ethnicity constraint. However, it comes negatively – albeit not at a significant effect – for the ethnic minority men in the cabinet. Where it picks up is for the *double-minorities*: a shift in political competition from no party in an authoritarian regime to 5.72 parties in a democracy can translate into a 5% – up to 8% – increase in the proportion of *double-hegemons*.

As an alternative way to interpret these conditional effects, the bottom two panels in Figure 4 consider the effects of shifting from a small ethnic minority group (one standard deviation below the mean: 2%) to a large one (one standard deviation above the mean: 57.2%) – given that political competition is low (i.e., 0 parties; see bottom left panel) or high (i.e., 5.72 parties; see bottom right panel). Changes in ethnic minority group size have no significant effect on the proportion of women in the cabinet. But this is only the case for the gender-only minorities. This is in stark contrast to the findings in Arriola and Johnson (2014). Instead, what matters – intuitively – is that as the ethnic minority group size increases, the proportion of ethnic minorities in the cabinet increases as well. However, whether it is just (1) ethnic minority men or (2) ethnic minority men *and women* that increase depends on the level of political competition. When competition is minimal, it is strictly about the ethnicity-only minorities (about 16% increase). However, when there is competition – and a lot of it – we see an increase in *double-minorities* as well (on average about 19%). In short, in politically competitive environments, large ethnic minority groups do indeed hold more portfolios in the cabinet, although the portfolios are not monopolized by one gender.

Next, we consider the effects of popular norms. It is possible a minority group – even if it is small – has a large ally population. Demands need not come just from the minority group; *double-hegemons* can also force chief executives to cobble together inclusive cabinets. To consider this, we rerun the same set of seemingly unrelated regressions from before, but this time we switch out the political competition measures for popular norms. We start with the measure of public attitudes from WVS.

The results (Appendix 3E; Model 2) suggest that popular norms have a positive effect on gender-only minority proportions. This is to be expected; as more people hold gender equity attitudes, this would translate into more women in the cabinet – but only if the women are of the ethnic hegemon group. And while the effects are in a similar direction for ethnic minorities, they are not statistically significant. But what is interesting is that these popular norms – when conditioned on ethnic minority group size – have a positive and substantial effect on *double-minority* proportions.

We plot the marginal effects in Figure 5 to grasp the magnitude. Let us start with the top left panel – that is, when the ethnic minority group is small. Increasing popular norms have a significant and positive effect for both gender-only minorities and ethnicity-only minorities. However, the substantive effects for the former are smaller than those for the latter. Moreover, when it comes to the proportion for *double-minorities*, the effects are significantly negative. The story, however, is very different when the ethnic minority group

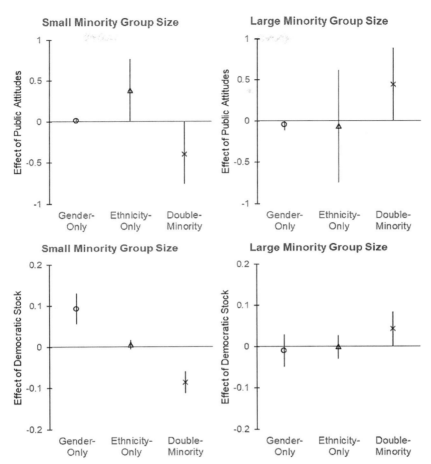

Figure 5 Marginal Effects Popular Norms on Cabinet Proportions across Minority Group Size

is large (top right panel): the conditional effects of popular norms are no longer significant. The nonsignificance is best illustrated by the effects for *ethnicity-only minorities*: a range from a 75% contraction to a 62% expansion! Where popular norms do matter is for *double-minorities*: a shift in popular norms can increase the proportion by 34%! This is the equivalent of going from zero to seven *double-minorities* in a twenty-person cabinet! This effect is huge.

Theoretically, we would expect attitudes toward diversity – even in the most socially liberal societies – to vary based on the individual's own identity and experiences. To consider this, we restrict the measure of public attitudes to consider only those of *double-hegemons*, the young (18–30 year olds), and the *double-hegemon* young. Empirically, the results remain largely robust (see

Appendix 3F). If anything, the effects are even more pronounced when we focus only on the *double-hegemons*. But here, we are cautious about generalizing these results given how few observations we have in the model and that the missing observations are not missing at random.

Given this reservation, we also look at the number of years a country has been a democracy. The intuition is that as democratic stock increases, there will be more tolerance of differences. The results suggest yes – as we see in the bottom panel of Figure 5 (see Appendix 3E; Model 3 for regression results). As democratic stock shifts from 0 years (one standard deviation below the mean) to 22 (one standard deviation above the mean), the proportion of *gender-only* minorities increases when the ethnic minority group is small (bottom left panel). This increase – of about 10% – is significant. And while there is no significant effect for ethnicity-only minorities, there is one – and it is a negative one – for *double-minorities*. Simply put, if there are norms for inclusion, but there are few ethnic minorities around, this translates into more ethnic hegemon women in the cabinet. The story is different, however, if the ethnic minority is large. As we see in the bottom right panel, there is no significant effect for the singular minorities. And instead, it is the *double-minorities* picking up the portfolios as popular norms of inclusion increase.

As a final consideration, we run a model where we include both political competition and popular norms (Appendix 3E; Model 4). The results suggest that political competition matters, but again, more so for gender-only minorities. When it comes to ethnic minorities, the effects are largely driven by popular norms. Taken together, these results are consistent with **Hypothesis 2.2** and highlight how popular norms matter for minority inclusion.

3.4 Discussion: Political Competition versus – and? – Popular Norms

While political competition and popular norms both matter for cabinet composition, these results raise several follow-up questions. First, which mechanism has a greater effect on whether minorities are in cabinets? Second, is one mechanism sufficient or are both necessary? And as an extension, if one is sufficient, is the presence of the second nominally superfluous or is it additive? To answer these questions, we rerun the same SUR model from before. This time, however, we include (1) the measure of political competition – that is, the *effective number of parties*; (2) one measure of popular norms – democratic stock given the larger N; and (3) an interaction between political competition and popular norms – with minority group size. Results can be found in Appendix 3E (Model 5).

To make sense of the three-way interaction, we plot the marginal effects (see Figure 6). In the top row, we look at the effects of political competition – given a small ethnic minority group and differing levels of popular norms in the first pair. As political competition increases, the substantive effects are small and often non-significant – even if there are strong popular norms. However, once we allow the ethnic minority group to be large, political competition has a negative effect on ethnicity-only minorities – *but a positive one for double-minorities* – when popular norms are strong. Simply put, we see a lot more *double-minorities* when (1) the ethnic minority population is large, (2) political competition is high, and (3) popular norms for inclusion are strong.

Next, in the bottom row, we look at the effects of popular norms – again, first given a small ethnic minority group but now given differing levels of political competition in the first pair. The two figures look very similar: increasing popular norms increases the proportion for gender-only minorities but decreases the proportion for ethnicity-only minorities. While the effects are nonsignificant for the *double-minorities*, it is interesting to note the average is positive, suggesting that even when there are ethnic minorities, there may be a tendency to include *double-minorities*.

The story, however, is remarkably different when the ethnic minority group is large. Even when there are popular norms for inclusion, in the absence of political competition, this manifests exclusively for men – including those from the ethnic minority group at almost 30%. The effects are statistically nondifferentiable from 0 for the *double-minorities*. But, in a setting where there is political competition – that is, where there are multiple political parties – we see the *double-minorities* picking up the portfolios at the expense of ethnic minority men.

These results suggest that (1) popular norms are necessary for the presence of *any* minority in the cabinet. Even if an ethnic minority group were large, and even if there was high political competition, in the absence of strong popular norms, we see either nonsignificant effects or very small substantive effects. It seems that of the two mechanisms, popular norms matter more than political competition for cabinet composition. These results also highlight how (2) both political competition and popular norms are necessary – and in fact interactive – for *double-minorities* in cabinets. This, of course, presupposes that there is also a large ethnic minority group. When this is the case, we see *double-minorities* picking up the extra portfolios at the expense of both single-minority groups. On average, the effect is 17%. In terms of substance, this is one *double-minority* per every six ministers!

When both mechanisms are present, the competing tensions to have both gender *and* ethnic minority ministers manifest as the cooptation of *double-minorities*. Giving portfolios to *double-minorities* serves two purposes. First, it allows the chief executive to instrumentally kill two birds with one stone. The

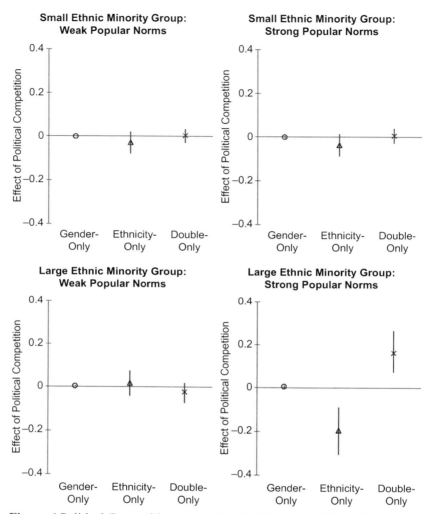

Figure 6 Political Competition versus Popular Norms on Cabinet Proportions

appointment of one *double-minority* is also the appointment of a gender minority *and* an ethnic minority. Second, the presence of *double-minorities* allows the chief executive to directly recognize said group as a distinct category. They are not simply an addition of their two minority identities but rather a unique third one. In any case, when the chief executive allocates portfolios to *double-minorities*, the proportion of gender and ethnic minorities both go up simultaneously as opposed to being in conflict.

These results echo findings from two strands of previous work. First, the identified patterns concerning the relative gains by *double-minorities* at the expense of ethnic minority men lend further support to work on the

Gender, Ethnicity, and Intersectionality in Cabinets

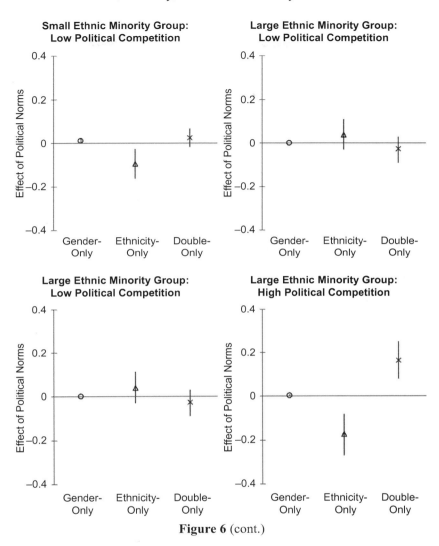

Figure 6 (cont.)

"complementarity advantage." Thus far, scholarship has provided evidence supporting the relative electoral advantage of ethnic minority women from mostly single-country case studies. Our analyses illustrate that the pattern seems to hold in a wider comparative context. Second, our results also corroborate work on cabinet selection. For example, Dowding and Dumont (2014) show that the executives of consolidated democracies – for example, the United Kingdom – are much more sensitive to public pressure when it comes to cabinet appointments than leaders of nondemocracies. Likewise, they show that minority group size and political competition play consequential roles in cabinet formation in countries like India. Again, our results speak to such works and lend additional comparative evidence in favor of these findings.

4 Minorities and Portfolio Prestige

When Finland declared independence in 1917, the first cabinet had eleven ministers. Among the eleven, there was one ethnic minority. Alexander Frey – the Deputy Internal Affairs Head[7] – was a Swede. The Swedish presence was intentional. The ongoing civil war against the Finnish Reds meant Prime Minister Pehr Evind Svinhufvud needed the support of the Swedish minority. The Swedes were not only the largest minority (at-the-time constituting 15% of the mainland population and the majority of Åland Islands), but they were also predominantly upper class – and thus ideologically predisposed to being anti-communists (Meinander 2020). Since Alexander Frey's appointment in 1917, barring a few periods, the Finnish cabinet has always included at least one ethnic Swede.

One decade after Alexander Frey in 1926, the Finnish cabinet welcomed its first woman: Miina Sillanpää as Deputy Social Affairs Minister. Despite how early the Finnish cabinets included both ethnic and gender minorities in government, it was not until 1990 that the cabinet had its first Swede woman: Märta Rehn. Rehn's appointment was significant not just because she was the first *double-minority*. Instead, her appointment as defense minister made her the first woman in that ministry *in the world* – a portfolio that had always been held by and thus associated with men (Barnes and O'Brien 2018; Escobar-Lemmon and Taylor-Robinson 2005; Krook and O'Brien 2012).

Ethnic minority women remain a fixture in the Finnish cabinet. When Sanna Marin was elected prime minister in 2019, newspaper headlines remarked on the gender equity and youth of her cabinet – for example, "Finland's new parliament is dominated by women under 35" (North 2019). Missing in the hype of who's who was another milestone: there were two ethnic Swede women in her cabinet: Anna-Maja Henriksson was the justice minister, and Li Andersson was the education minister – a highly coveted portfolio for ethnic minorities.

The Finland case highlights not just the diversity of ministers but the diversity of portfolio prestige. While the previous section demonstrated when we would expect to see minorities in cabinets, there was an underlying assumption that all cabinet portfolios are theoretically equal. Yet, this is far from reality. Certain

---

[7] Countries vary in whether deputy ministers are considered full-fledged members of the cabinet. Moreover, this variation can also fluctuate across administrations. Here, we defer to the official sources: if deputy ministers are listed as part of the cabinet by a country in a given year, we consider them full-fledged members. This ensures we apply the same coding rule equally to all countries over time.

portfolios are more prestigious – for example, defense (Barnes and O'Brien 2018; Meng and Payne 2022) and finance (Armstrong et al. 2022). Conversely, there are others that are simply less flashy even if they are widely recognized as important – for example, education (Apfeld and Liu 2021) and health (Selway 2015a). Having more minorities in a cabinet can have a token feel if they are consistently relegated to less prestigious portfolios.

In this section, we test not just whether politically competitive states and states with popular norms in favor of inclusion have more minorities in their cabinets but also whether minorities are being assigned to portfolios of higher or lower prestige. The intuition is that when chief executives are constrained, they cannot afford to simply dole out token portfolios. At some point, they must coopt the minority group by giving them a larger and louder voice.

4.1 Research Design

We return to our *country-year-minister* dataset (N=91,000). We are now interested in the relative positions of different ministries. To measure prestige, we employ two different strategies. One is an objective ordered rank measure; the other is a subjective categorical measure.

Objective Ordered Rank: Recall, we scraped the printed annual versions of the *Europa World Yearbook*. We used the *Europa World Yearbook* because many of the alternative sources (e.g., Bank's *Political Handbook of the World*) list cabinet ministers alphabetically in English per their ministry's name. The left panel in Figure 7 shows the CIA *World Factbook* entry for Romania 2007. Note that after the prime minister and the deputy prime minister, the ministries are listed alphabetically with administrative reform and agriculture in the third and fourth spots, respectively. Transportation is fifth from the bottom.

Conversely, the *Europa World Yearbook* lists cabinet ministries in the order officially published by the government in that year. The order could be alphabetical (e.g., pre-Taliban Afghanistan), it could be based on the date of the ministry's creation (e.g., the United States), it could be based on the minister's seniority (e.g., Singapore during the first generation), or it could be based on coalition bargaining (e.g., Romania). Regardless of why the ministries are listed in a particular order, the order is inherently the product of some political decision – whether explicit or not. As it is a list, it fundamentally suggests a hierarchy where those at the top are more prestigious than those listed at the bottom. As a validity check, we observe that the prime minister (or the equivalent) is always first; it is never last. Likewise, the deputy prime minister frequently follows the prime minister – and they are never in the bottom half of the list.

Source: CIA World Factbook

Prime Min.	Calin Popescu-TARICEANU
Dep. Prime Min. for Culture, Education, & European Integration	
Min. of Admin. Reform & Interior	Cristian DAVID
Min. of Agriculture & Rural Development	Decebal Traian REMES
Min. of Communication & Information Technology	Iuliu WINKLER
Min. of Culture & Religious Affairs	Adrian IORGULESCU
Min. of Defense	Teodor Viorel MELESCANU
Min. of Development, Public Works, & Housing	Laszlo BORBELY
Min. of Economy & Finance	Varujan VOSGANIAN
Min. of Education, Youth, & Research	Cristian ADOMNITEI
Min. of Environment & Sustainable Development	Attila KORODI
Min. of Foreign Affairs	Adrian CIOROIANU
Min. of Health	Eugen NICOLAESCU
Min. of Justice	Tudor CHIUARIU
Min. of Labor, Social Solidarity, & Family	Paul PACURARU
Min. for Small & Medium-Sized Enterprises, Trade, Tourism & Freelance Professions	Ovidiu SILAGHI
Min. of Transport	Ludovic ORBAN
Min.-Del. for Relations With Parliament	Mihai Alexandru VOICU
Governor, National Bank of Romania	Mugur ISARESCU
Ambassador to the US	
Permanent Representative to the UN, New York	Mihnea MOTOC

Source: Europa World Yearbook

Prime Minister: CĂLIN CONSTANTIN ANTON POPESCU-TĂRICEANU (NLP).

Minister of State, responsible for Co-ordination of Activities in the Fields of Culture, Education and European Integration: BELA MARKO (DAHR).

Minister of Foreign Affairs: ADRIAN CIOROIANU (NLP).

Minister of Justice: TUDOR CHIUARIU (NLP).

Minister of the Interior and Administrative Reform: TUDOR CHIUARIU (NLP).

Minister of the Economy and Finance: VARUJAN VOSGANIAN (NLP).

Minister of Defence: TEODOR MELESCANU (NLP).

Minister of Labour, the Family and Equal Opportunities: PAUL PĂCURARU (NLP).

Minister of Small and Medium-Sized Enterprises, Trade, Tourism and the Liberal Professions: OVIDIU SILAGHI (NLP).

Minister of Agriculture and Rural Development: DECEBAL TRAIAN REMEȘ (NLP).

Minister of Transport: LUDOVIC ORBAN (NLP).

Minister of Education, Research and Youth: CRISTIAN ADOMNITEI (NLP).

Minister of Culture and Religious Affairs: ADRIAN IORGULESCU (NLP).

Minister of Public Health: EUGEN NICOLĂESCU (NLP).

Minister of Development, Public Works and Housing: LÁSZLÓ BORBÉLY (DAHR).

Minister of Communications and Information Technology: ZSOLT NAGY (DAHR).

Minister of the Environment and Sustainable Development: EUGEN NICOLĂESCU (DAHR).

Minister-delegate for Relations with Parliament: MIHAI ALEXANDRU VOICU (NLP).

Figure 7 Example of Cabinet Listings (Romania 2007)

The right panel in Figure 7 shows the cabinet listing for Romania 2007 in the *Europa World Yearbook*.[8] When we look at the *Europa World Yearbook* listing, the agriculture and transportation ministers are (1) in the middle of the list and (2) sequential to each other. This suggests the two ministers are of middle rank within the larger cabinet. Moreover, the two are roughly of equal rank. This is in stark contrast to the CIA's *World Factbook*. If we had used these alternative sources, the agriculture minister would consistently appear near the top across countries and over time, and the transport minister would regularly be near the bottom. Using these lists would have resulted in a linguistically driven erroneous conclusion about the prestige of cabinet ranks. In short, we argue the list order – whatever rubric the government uses – matters.

With this ordering, we construct an index of ministry ranks held by *double-hegemons*, gender-only minorities, ethnicity-only minorities, and *double-minorities*. We use the following formula:

$$\frac{\sum_{n=1}^{k}(k+1-n)^2 * Group}{\sum_{n=1}^{k} n^2}$$

The formula considers each ministry held by ministers of each group – weighted by its cabinet rank. For example, let us assume the prime minister was a *double-hegemon* (rank=1 in a cabinet with k ministries). He would be weighted k^2. Conversely, a *double-hegemon* in the k-th ministry would have a rank of 1^2. We square the ranks to reward higher placements. We then sum the weights held by all *double-hegemons* in the cabinet and divide it by the total number of possible weights. A value of 0 (minimum) would indicate a cabinet with no *double-hegemons* – in *any* rank, and a value of 1 (maximum) would suggest a cabinet where *all* the ministers were *double-hegemons*. We repeat this formula for gender-only minorities, ethnicity-only minorities, and *double-minorities*.

Subjective Power Scores: Focusing on the objective ordered rank, however, assumes the prestige gap between the first two ministries listed is the same as the last two ministries at the bottom. Yet, this is not subjectively the case. Ministries are often conceptualized in groups or tiers. Selway (2015a: 103) notes that in Thailand, there is a "ministry pecking order based on the size of the budget and ease of [political] manipulation." As an alternative, to measure the subjective rank of ministries, we follow a strategy used by Krook and O'Brien (2012) when they created the *Gender Power Score* (GPS). First, they use Escobar-Lemmon and Taylor-Robinson's (2005) rubric for identifying the prestige of

---

[8] Some names do not match across the two listings; these are the result of when each list was published in that year.

cabinets in Latin America – that is, whether they are high, medium, or low prestige (see Appendix 4A). Portfolios with high visibility and substantial policy influence (e.g., defense and finance) are of *high* prestige; those with less visibility and influence but still possessing financial resources (e.g., agriculture and education), *medium* prestige; and those with minimal resources and visibility (e.g., culture and tourism), *low* prestige.

Krook and O'Brien (2012) apply the cabinet prestige rubric to a global sample and then consider the gendered nature of the portfolios (see Appendix 4B). Portfolios are considered *masculine* if they have a public element and are often associated with men (e.g., defense and foreign affairs); *feminine* if they have a private, family element and are linked to women (e.g., education and youth); and *neutral* if neither (e.g., environment and justice). With this information, GPS is calculated as follows:

GPS $= [(\%High \times 3) + (\%Medium \times 2) + (\%Low \times 1) +$
$(\%Masculine \times 3) + (\%Neutral \times 2) + (\%Feminine \times 1)] \times \%Women$

where (1) the percentage of *high* prestige portfolios held by women is weighted by 3, (2) the percentage of *medium* prestige portfolios held by women is weighted by 2, (3) the percentage of *low* prestige portfolios held by women is weighted by 1, (4) the percentage of *masculine* portfolios held by women is weighted by 3, (5) the percentage of *neutral* portfolios held by women is weighted by 2, and (6) the percentage of *feminine* portfolios held by women is weighted by 1 – and then summed up and weighted collectively by the percentage of women in the entire cabinet. Altogether, a cabinet composed completely of women would score a maximum of 12, and conversely, a cabinet with a minimum score of 0 is one without any women.

Using GPS as a starting template, we make one modification and two extensions. The first modification is that since there are additional ministerial posts that are not identified in Krook and O'Brien (2012) – for example, Ministry for the Coordination of Activities in the Fields of Culture, Education, and European Integration (*Romania-2007*) and the Ministry of Psychological Warfare (*South Vietnam-1965*) – we consider everything of medium prestige unless it explicitly matches an identified ministry of high or low prestige.

Second, Krook and O'Brien (2012) only focus on the gendered type of the portfolio – that is, whether it was masculine, neutral, or feminine. As an extension, we create a similar typology for the ethnic type of the portfolio: *hegemon, neutral,* or *minority*. The two lists are largely the same except we consider "women's affair" as neutral when it comes to

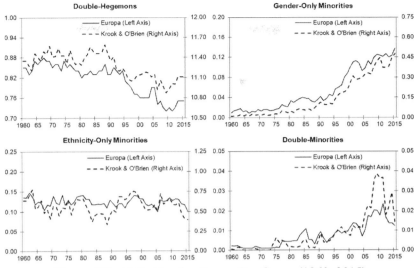

Figure 8 Portfolio Prestige Scores Per Group (1960–2015)

ethnicity; and likewise, "minority affairs" is considered minority when it comes to ethnicity. With this typology, we then create an *Ethnicity Power Score* (EPS). Third, with the GPS and EPS, we can then identify a *Double-Minority Power Score* (DMPS). We consider a portfolio to be a "minority intersecting" portfolio if it is identified as either feminine *or* ethnic minority. Conversely, a portfolio is coded as a "hegemon intersecting" if it is both masculine *and* ethnic hegemon.

The Europa *World Yearbook*'s ordered rank and Krook and O'Brien's power scores are highly correlated: 0.80 for the *double-hegemons* and a 0.66 for the *double-minorities*. Figure 8 shows the portfolio prestige for each group between 1960 and 2015 for both measures. As a reminder, the maximum for the *Europa World Yearbook* is a 1.0; and for the Krook and O'Brien power score, a 12. We see similar patterns for both measures. The prestige held by the *double-hegemon* overshadows that of all other minority groups, although the prestige has dropped over time. The prestige for gender-only minorities has steadily increased since the 1980s. The same cannot be said, however, for ethnicity-only minorities. Their pattern looks very much like a healthy electrocardiogram reading: It can fluctuate wildly from one period to the next, but overall, the slope is a flat line. And finally, while *double-minorities* have by far the least prestigious portfolios, there is a significant difference over time with both measures.

4.2 Empirical Evidence

Using both measures of cabinet rank, we first test whether governments facing political competition and popular norms have fewer *double-hegemons* in higher prestige portfolios. We use the same measure of political competition from before (*effective number of parties*) and run a series of ordinary least squares regressions – with cabinet prestige of *double-hegemons* as the dependent variable. We show the regression results in Table 4. As we see in Models 1 and 4, political competition has a significant – *and negative* – effect when it comes to the portfolio prestige of *double-hegemons*. This corroborates **Hypothesis 3.1**: When minority groups can mobilize – as evident by the presence of many political parties – they demand and extract not just more portfolios but more prestigious portfolios. This is the case regardless of whether we measure prestige using the *Europa World Yearbook* rank order measure or Krook and O'Brien's power score.

Next, we consider the effects of popular norms. In Models 2 and 5, we measure popular norms as public attitudes per WVS. Again, the results are consistent with our theoretical expectations in **Hypothesis 3.2**: When there are strong norms surrounding the inclusion of diversity, this translates into *double-hegemons* relinquishing more prestigious portfolios. The marginal effects are sizable: contractions for *double-hegemons* can vary between 9% (Krook and O'Brien) to 17% (*Europa World Yearbook*).

But recall, one concern we have had with the WVS measure is the nonrandom selection of *country-years*. There is a heavier bias toward democracies than authoritarian regimes; likewise, there is more bias toward countries in Europe than Asia. This large substantive effect could be an artificial product of sample truncation. As an alternative, we consider democratic stock. In Models 3 and 6, we see the concerned coefficients are much, much smaller. Moreover, in one of the models, the effect is not statistically significant, thus suggesting that while popular norms may translate into more minorities in cabinets, it does not necessarily guarantee them having the more prestigious portfolios.

Having established that political competition constrains governments to give up (some) of the more prestigious portfolios to minorities, we now identify *which* minority groups are receiving the positions. We run the same seemingly unrelated regression models from before – except this time we focus on the weighted proportions for each group (regressions reported in Appendix 4C for *Europa World Yearbook* and Appendix 4D for Krook and O'Brien). The results mirror previous findings: a large ethnic minority group in a politically competitive environment can constrain chief executives to not only appoint more *double-minorities* but to appoint them to portfolios of higher prestige than

Table 4 Effects of Political Competition and Popular Norms on Portfolio Prestige for Double-Hegemons

| | *Europa World Yearbook* Ordered Rank ||||| Krook and O'Brien Power Score ||
	Political Competition	Popular Norms: Attitudes	Popular Norms: Stock	Political Competition	Popular Norms: Attitudes	Popular Norms: Stock
	(1)	(2)	(3)	(4)	(5)	(6)
Ethnic Minority Size	−0.109 (0.159)	0.386 (0.156)[‡]	−0.147 (0.184)	0.037 (0.070)	−0.041 (0.113)	0.008 (0.052)
Effective # Parties	−0.003 (0.001)[‡]			−0.001 (0.001)*		
Attitudes: WVS		−0.172 (0.098)*			−0.089 (0.045)*	
# Years Democracy			0.001 (0.000)[‡]			−0.000 (0.000)
Constant	0.412 (0.023)[‡]	−0.582 (0.143)[‡]	0.449 (0.175)[†]	0.440 (0.040)[‡]	0.216 (0.021)[‡]	0.502 (0.082)[‡]
N	2910	677	2349	2910	677	2349
R^2	0.849	0.857	0.842	0.909	0.955	0.899
Root MSE	0.081	0.084	0.081	0.042	0.037	0.041

Notes. Dependent variable: "Portfolio Prestige of *Double-Hegemons*." Results are from OLS regressions with GDP per capita, colonial dummy, region dummy, lagged dependent variable, country fixed effects, and decade fixed effects. Standard errors in parentheses. *p≤0.10; [†]p≤0.05; [‡]p≤0.01.

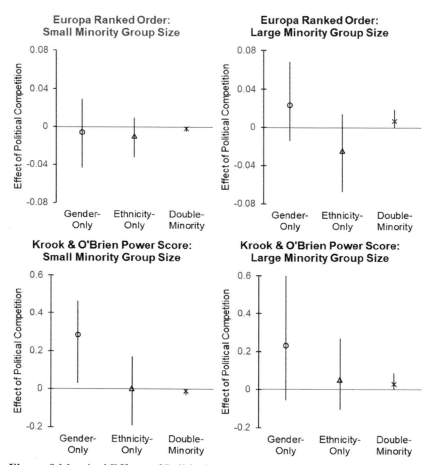

Figure 9 Marginal Effects of Political Competition on Portfolio Prestige across Minority Group Size

their counterparts in less competitive environments. This effect – statistically significant at the 0.01 level – is robust for both the *Europa World Yearbook*'s objective ordered rank and Krook and O'Brien's subjective power score.

To get a better sense of this pattern, we plot marginal effects in Figure 9. The top row uses the *Europa World Yearbook* measure. In the top left-hand panel, we see that when the ethnic minority population is small, political competition has no significant effect on minority cabinet prestige. This is the case for both gender-only and ethnicity-only minorities. And while the effect is significant (and negative) for *double-minorities*, the substantive effect is extremely small. Simply put, political competition has no effect on minority portfolio prestige – *but only when the ethnic minority population is small*.

Gender, Ethnicity, and Intersectionality in Cabinets   51

Table 5 Gender Power Scores (GPS) in a Hypothetical 20-Person Cabinet

	Prestige			Gender Type			GPS
	High ($N=5$)	Medium ($N=5$)	Low ($N=10$)	Masculine ($N=5$)	Neutral ($N=10$)	Feminine ($N=5$)	
0	0	0	0	0	0	0	0
	0	0	1	0	0	1	0.02
1	0	1	0	0	0	1	0.03
	1	0	0	1	0	0	0.06
	0	1	1	0	1	1	0.09
2	0	2	0	0	2	0	0.12
	1	1	0	1	0	1	0.18
	0	1	2	0	2	1	0.18
3	0	2	1	0	1	2	0.23
	1	1	1	1	1	1	**0.32**
	0	3	1	0	3	1	0.40
4	1	2	1	1	2	1	0.54
	1	3	0	1	3	0	0.60
20	5	5	10	5	10	5	12.0

The story is different if the ethnic minority population is large. Political competition still has no significant effect for either of the two single-minorities. However, it now has a positive and significant effect for *double-minorities*. But the substantive effect is still quite small – on average at about 0.01, with a maximum of about 0.02. This is the equivalent of having either (1) two *double-minorities* holding the two least prestigious portfolios or (2) one *double-minority* holding a moderately prestigious portfolio.

This general pattern holds even when we consider prestige using Krook and O'Brien's power score: (1) when the ethnic minority group is small, political competition has a negative effect for *double-minorities*; (2) when the ethnic minority group is large, political competition has a positive effect for *double-minorities*; but (3) in both cases, the magnitude of the effect is quite small. There is one interesting difference worth noting, however. As the bottom left-hand panel shows, when the ethnic minority group is small, political competition can translate into significantly more prestigious portfolios for the gender-only minorities. To grasp what a change of 0.30 means in this case, consider Table 5, which shows a range of possible gender power scores across different portfolio assignments in a hypothetical twenty-person cabinet. Simply put, political competition matters for portfolio prestige – but only for some minority groups.

What about popular norms? Are governments more likely to dole out higher prestige portfolios to *double-minorities* when there is general support for minority inclusion in the government? The answer is yes. The coefficients for the interaction term (*Minority* × *Norms*) are significant and sizable regardless of whether we measure popular norms with public attitudes (Model 2) or democratic stock (Model 3) – and regardless of whether we measure portfolio prestige with *Europa World Yearbook*'s objective ordered rank (Appendix 4C) or Krook and O'Brien's subjective power score (Appendix 4D). Substantive representation for *double-minorities* is more likely when there is a large ethnic minority population and when there is general support for their inclusion.

Figure 10 illustrates these effects. The top row uses the WVS measure of popular norms. Let us first focus on the cases where the ethnic minority group is small. When the public believes in gender equity and is tolerant of ethnic differences, this has (1) a positive and significant effect on portfolio prestige for *gender-only minorities* – regardless of whether we use the *Europa World Yearbook* or the Krook and O'Brien measure; (2) a positive – although not robust – effect on portfolio prestige for *ethnicity-only minorities*; and (3) a negative and significant effect on portfolio prestige for *double-minorities*. In short, it seems we observe the zero-sum dynamic between gender and ethnicity noted by Jensenius (2016), Arriola and Johnson (2015), and Pierskalla et al. (2021).

This dynamic, however, changes if the ethnic minority group is large (57.2%, i.e., one standard deviation above the mean). We see less evidence of a tension between gender and ethnicity. In both the *Europa World Yearbook* and Krook and O'Brien measures, the average effects for popular norms are negative. And even then, they are not significant. Instead, it seems that if there are major substantive, significant, and positive effects for popular norms, they are manifesting for *double-minorities*. This suggests that (1) when no ethnic group commands a majority of the population and (2) the public strongly believes in the inclusion of women and ethnic minorities, we should see large(r) numbers of *double-minorities* in higher-ranking portfolios in the cabinet.

Next, we pivot the focus from public attitudes to democratic stock. The inclusion of four times as many *country-year* observations is evident in the much smaller confidence intervals. First, when the ethnic minority group is small, this results in (1) the gender-only minorities getting a much larger share of the more prestigious portfolios – at the expense of both (2) the ethnicity-only minorities and (3) the *double-minorities*. We see – yet again – the tension between gender and ethnicity. Moreover, what is remarkable is that where there is no tension – that is, when it is about *double-minorities* – the results are robust and significant, but the magnitude is nominally a 0.

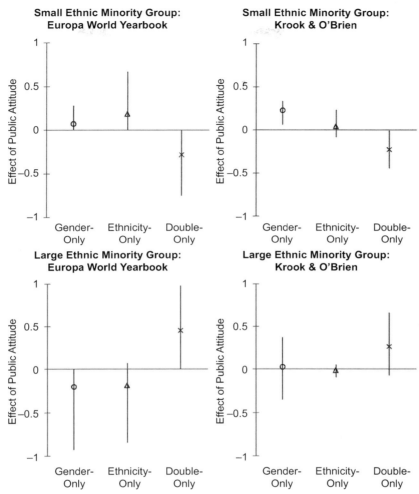

Figure 10 Marginal Effects of Popular Norms on Portfolio Prestige across Minority Group Size

Next, we see no significant effects whatsoever when the ethnic minority group is large. This nonsignificance is robust across all minority groups; it is also robust across the different portfolio prestige measures. There are two explanations for this. The first is about measurement: specifically, democratic stock is a less-than-ideal measure of popular norms. While this is certainly a possibility, the fact that the same measure yielded results that are consistent with the "small ethnic group size" panel suggests measurement is not the culprit. This brings us to the other explanation. While a population may believe in the inclusion of diversity, this does not necessarily translate into prestigious

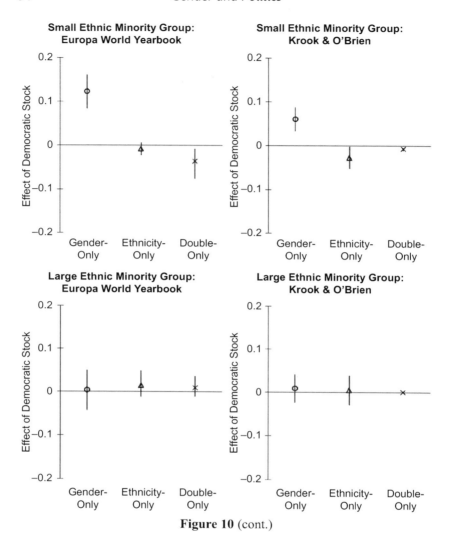

Figure 10 (cont.)

portfolios for minorities. The fact that the marginal effects using WVS are also mostly nonsignificant lends support to this explanation. Simply put, just because there are norms dictating inclusion does not mean governments will include that diversity well.

4.3 Discussion: Symbolism versus Significance

In this section, we find that it is the popular norms mechanism that is associated with minorities in higher-ranking cabinet posts. Conversely, governments in politically competitive environments are not necessarily more inclined to have minorities in more prestigious portfolios – even though they may have more minorities in the cabinet. But in either case, the magnitude of the effects is disproportionally and discouragingly small.

This is not to say that less prestigious portfolios do not matter. Descriptive representation is important: having minorities in portfolios that are traditionally associated with minorities – such as women's affairs (for gender) and minority affairs (for ethnicity) – means policies are more likely to be congruent with the preferences and needs of said group. Yet, when minorities are relegated to *only* these portfolios – as opposed to ones that have broader implications for the general population – it suggests their ability to advocate for their minority group is limited. For example, consider the logistics of allowing gender minorities into certain military units. This change is one that cannot be done simply by the Minister of Women's Affairs. It requires the support from the Minister of Defense. When a minister in a country with almost gender parity in its legislature approached her counterpart in the Defense Ministry about gender inclusivity in the military, she was rebuked along the lines, "We already gave you gender mainstreaming in the legislature, in the board room, and in everything else. Why must you come for the military?" (Interview, June 8, 2022). Likewise, imagine if an ethnic minority needs better road access to maintain agricultural lands. This cannot be done simply by a Minister of Minority Affairs. They need to coordinate with the Minister of Transportation. Yet, if the Minister of Transportation is simply going to trivialize these efforts along the lines of, "We already gave you a portfolio. We already allow you to wear your [ethnic] clothing. Don't be so demanding" (Interview, May 2, 2022), this can limit what a minority minister can do. Simply put, when minorities are only in minority-related portfolios, it limits their capacity to influence policy and administer resources.

The results suggest significant barriers in other ways. Even when there are minorities in cabinets and even when they are in higher prestige portfolios, the numbers are still quite low. In particular, when it comes to *double-minorities*, their numbers and portfolio prestige are the lowest of the three minority groups. Consider how Sanna Marin's cabinet in Finland was touted for its diversity. Yet, there were still only two *double-minorities*. Likewise, Jacinda Arden's 2020 cabinet in New Zealand – despite being the most inclusive to date – had only five *double-minorities* out of thirty. This is not meant as a criticism of Marin's or Arden's efforts at inclusion. Instead, they are examples of (1) how two of the most inclusive cabinets happened in places where popular norms for inclusion were high but where the ethnic hegemon group is still comfortably in the majority (Finland: 91.5% Finnish; New Zealand: 65.6% White European descent). The two cases also illustrate that while political competition and popular norms – whether singularly or collectively – can drive portfolio proportions, their effects on portfolio prestige are more limited.

5 Minorities in Cabinets in Four Cases

In this section, we examine how political competition and popular norms affect cabinet composition in four cases: China, the United Kingdom, the Soviet Union/Russia, and India. Figure 11 shows the proportions of *double-hegemons* in each of the four countries over time. What is remarkable is the spatial and temporal variation. In China, *double-hegemons* were dominant at the founding of the People's Republic of China (PRC; 1949) and continue to be. This constant monopoly of power is in stark contrast to its two geographical neighbors. First, in the Soviet Union, the proportion of *double-hegemons* held stable at just above 60% before increasing in the Gorbachev years (1985–1991). The number dropped with the collapse of the Soviet Union – despite losing fourteen republics (i.e., large minority populations). Since then, the numbers have returned to historic highs. Second, in India, while *double-hegemons* were the plurality group in the cabinet at independence (1947), their numbers have oscillated wildly over the years. Finally, the pattern in the United Kingdom is one of constancy for *double-hegemons* until the mid-1990s, when we see drops. This section contextualizes these patterns – with particular attention to the minority ministers.

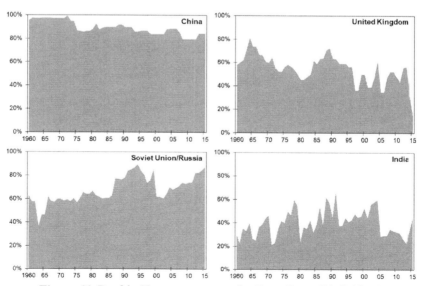

Figure 11 *Double-Hegemons* across the Four Cases (% Cabinet)

Gender, Ethnicity, and Intersectionality in Cabinets

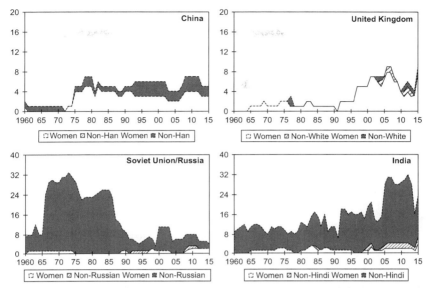

Figure 12 Minority Ministers in the Four Cases (# Ministers)

We focus on these four cases for two reasons. First, they vary in which minority group(s) is accommodated in the cabinet – if at all. As we see in Figure 12, in one case (China), the *double-hegemons* have held on to the monopoly of power; in another case (the United Kingdom), we see the inclusion of gender-only minorities – at a rate much higher than other minority groups; in the third case (the Soviet Union/Russia), co-optation manifests more around ethnicity-only minorities; and in the fourth case (India), we see inclusion of all three minority groups.

Second, these four cases lend themselves to a controlled comparison (Slater and Ziblatt 2013). In a controlled comparison where the dependent variable varies across cases, an alternative explanation should ideally have the same value across all the cases. When this is not possible, what matters is that where they are different, they have similar dependent variable outcomes – thus logically removing this alternative explanation (and likewise where they are similar, they have different outcomes).

For example, one alternative explanation could be about regime type; that is, democracies have more diverse cabinets. As we see in Table 6, two of the four countries are democracies; the other two are not (albeit, Russia enjoyed a brief period of democracy in the 1990s). And while it is true that the country with the least diverse cabinet is authoritarian (China) and the one with the most diverse cabinet is a democracy (India), it is not the case that authoritarian regimes are systematically less likely to have minorities in their cabinets. In fact, from an ethnicity standpoint, Soviet/Russian cabinets have been more diverse than British ones.

Table 6 A Controlled Comparison Design

	China	United Kingdom	Soviet Union/ Russia	India
Minorities in Cabinet	None: *Double-Hegemons*	Gender-Only Minorities	Ethnicity-Only Minorities	All including *Double-Minorities*
Regime Type	Non-Democracy	Democracy	Non-Democracy	Democracy
Economy ($t = 0$)	Poverty Levels: High	Poverty Levels: Medium	Poverty Levels: High	Poverty Levels: High
Economy (2015)	HDI: High	HDI: Very High	HDI: High	HDI: Medium
Colonial Legacy	None: Colonizer	None: Colonizer	None: Colonizer	British
Region	Asia: East	Europe: West	Asia: Central, West; Europe: East	Asia: South
Women Suffrage	1949	1918	1917	1950
Hegemon Ethnic Group	Han (91%)[1]	White (80%)[2]	Russian (51%)[3]; (78%)[4]	Hindi (44%)[2]
Political Competition	Low	High	High	High
Popular Norms	Weak	Strong: Gender	Strong: Ethnicity	Strong: Ethnicity > Gender

Notes: [1] 2020 Census. [2] 2011 Census. [3] 1989 Census. [4] 2010 Census.

Another explanation could be about economic development. Yet, what we see is that three of the cases started out quite poor (revolutions are good at depleting coffers), but three are considered by different metrics as having high human development today. Regardless of how we measure development and conceptualize modernization, we see the limits of this explanation. If increasing wealth is supposed to facilitate tolerance per Lipset (1959), we should observe the most drastic changes in China. Yet that is precisely the case where we see no minority ministers. Likewise, the United Kingdom is the case with the lowest poverty level at the start of the analysis and has continued to grow in wealth. Yet ethnic minority representation has paled in comparison with either the Soviet Union/Russia or India. And in fact, the country with the most diversity in its cabinet is the one that started poor and is still – by almost all metrics – the weakest economically.

Cabinet composition also cannot be due to colonial legacy. For starters, three of the cases were at one point empires themselves. And while India – a British colony – has the most diverse cabinet, it is not simply a story about the British

Gender, Ethnicity, and Intersectionality in Cabinets

establishing better governing institutions than their continental European counterparts. In fact, the British had considerable influence in China during the Qing Dynasty following the Opium Wars. Yet, whatever British values were adopted by Imperial China, it does not seem to have translated into cabinet diversity post-1949. And while the United Kingdom itself has done relatively well with respect to gender diversity in cabinets, this diversity has been mostly White. Its record with ethnic minority representation leaves much to be desired.

In a similar vein, whether there are minorities in the cabinet cannot be due to some larger regional effect. Geographically, two of the cases are in Asia – one with the most exclusive cabinet and one with the most inclusive. And the other two cases are in Europe – albeit Russia spans both Europe and Asia. Moreover, all four countries are (have been) major powers regionally – if not globally. Admittedly, there may be differences between East Asia and South Asia, between Western Europe and Eastern Europe. But focusing on these subregional differences risks parroting Huntington's clash of civilization explanation, which is not only fatalistic but also static. Put differently, civilizational explanations cannot explain the dynamic, over-time changes in cabinet composition.

Alternative explanations that focus on the minority groups themselves are likewise limited. If women's suffrage is a proxy for when they started to have a political voice, we see that the Soviet Union/Russia was in fact the first of the four cases to enfranchise women – yet the number of women in cabinets has been abysmal. And while women in China and India were afforded the right to vote decades later, given state history those dates were the earliest point possible – that is, at independence. In fact, suffrage for women in China, the Soviet Union/Russia, and India all happened nominally at the same stage of state-building. Yet, the presence of women in cabinets – whether from the outset or today – cannot be any more different.

What about the size of the ethnic minority? Here, we see some evidence to corroborate **Corollary 1 and Corollary 2:** ethnic minorities are more likely to be present in cabinets as their size increases. In China – despite having fifty-five officially recognized ethnic minorities – the Hans constitute a staggering 91% of the population. Likewise, in the United Kingdom, the Whites – which admittedly is in and of itself a heterogeneous grouping that includes the Scottish, Welsh, and Irish minorities – are 80% of the population. Conversely, in the other two cases, the ethnic hegemons barely constitute a majority – if at all (India). In short, the dominance of the ethnic hegemons makes it difficult for ethnic minorities to extract cabinet portfolios. We will see a similar dynamic in the Soviet Union/Russia case once the Soviet Union collapses, leaving the ethnic Russians a supermajority of the population (78%).

Table 7 The Firsts in the Four Cases

	China	United Kingdom	Soviet Union/ Russia	India
Hegemon Ethnic Group	Han (91%)[1]	White (80%)[2]	Russian (51%)[3]; (78%)[4]	Hindi (44%)[2]
First in Cabinet				
Women	1949: Shi Liang (*Justice*) and Dequan Li (*Health*)	1929: Margaret Bondfield (*Labor*)	1917: Alexandra Kollantai (*Social Welfare*)	1947: Amrit Kaur (*Health*)
Ethnic Minorities	1949: Daiyuan Teng (*Railway*)	2002: Paul Boateng (*Treasury*)	1917 (N=4)	1947 (N=10) including Deputy Prime Minister
Double-Minorities	None	2003: Valerie Amos (*International Development*)	1917: Alexandra Kollantai (*Social Welfare*)	1947: Amrit Kaur (*Health*)

Notes. [1] 2020 Census. [2] 2011 Census. [3] 1989 Census. [4] 2010 Census.

Given this discussion, we are left with our two explanatory variables: **political competition** and **popular norms**. And as we see, the two variables vary across the four cases – with both being absent in China. And while political competition is high *and* popular norms for inclusion are strong in all the other three cases, there is variation as to *which* group – as we see in Table 7. In the remainder of this section, we discuss how (1) political competition *and* popular norms (2) for both women and ethnic minorities constrain the chief executives with cabinet compositions (3) in each of the four cases.

5.1 Monopolization of the *Double-Hegemons* in Chinese Cabinets

Contemporary China is a multiethnic republic with a majority Han population (91%). While there are fifty-five officially recognized ethnic minorities – with the largest being the Zhuang (*Bourau*, 1.4%), Hui (Chinese Muslims), Manchu, Uyghur, Miao, Yi, Tujia, Tibetan, and Mongols – the government has prioritized the "culturalization" (Ma 2006) and "Hanification" (Liu and Peters 2017) of ethnic minority groups (Ma 2006).

In the 1950s, the PRC attempted to mirror the Soviet Union's *korenizatsiya* (indigenization) policy for managing ethnic diversity (discussed further in the

Soviet Union/Russian section below). The Chinese government introduced the Regional Ethnic Autonomy System to preserve the cultural integrity of minority groups (Ma 2006). Ethnic minorities had the rights to learn their native languages, cultural expression, a dedicated territory, and roles in the government. Five minority groups in particular (Zhuang, Hui, Uyghur, Tibetan, and Mongols) formed ethnic autonomous regions at the provincial level. These efforts, however, were set against a larger need to fit these groups into the Chinese political system. At the time, the government lacked the economic resources to institute any pro-Han (Mandarin) policy in the post-civil war environment (Dreyer 2003). Consequently, ethnic minorities gained greater say in their governance. Simply put, the Chinese government lacked the capacity to assimilate or repress the minorities.

To ensure that these groups did not become a political threat, the Chinese Communist Party (CCP) afforded them "rents" in the form of limited cultural autonomy. These rents, however, did not translate to representation at the highest levels of government. While ethnic minorities posed enough of a threat – that is, were sufficiently mobilized – to make the Chinese government provide cultural autonomy, the political system was insufficiently competitive and popular norms of inclusion were absent, precluding representation at the highest levels of government.

Moreover, the limited cultural autonomy instituted by the CCP would not last. As China developed, and as state capacity increased, much of the initial ethnic autonomy from the 1950s was undone through forced assimilation policies (Dreyer 2003). As we see in Figure 12, cabinet appointments – at the central level – have been dominated by Han men. There have been very few minorities – whether gender and/or ethnicity – in the Chinese cabinet.

While ethnic minorities have had greater representation at the local and grass-root levels, their appointment at the national level has been scarce and subject to complex ideological considerations. For example, in the first three decades of the PRC (1949–1979), ethnic minorities who made it to the core leadership circle were almost always those who not only paid allegiance to the CCP but also contributed to military operations during the 1937–1945 Sino-Japanese War and the 1945–1949 Chinese Civil War (News of the Communist Party of China 1956). These included Teng Daiyuan, an ethnic Miao. In 1949 – from the outset – Teng was appointed Minister of Railways. And then there was Ulanhu, an ethnic Mongol. His resume included vice premier (1954–1966), Minister of the State Ethnic Affairs Commission (1954–1966), Minister of the United Front Work Department (1977–1982), and vice president of China (1983–1988). To date, Ulanhu is the highest-ranking minority official in PRC history.[9]

---

[9] www.xinhuanet.com/focus/xiangguan/02022711.htm

Ulanhu's placement into a high-ranking cabinet position was not an accident. Popular norms projected – sometimes forcibly – Han culture onto the other ethnic groups. For ethnic minorities who wanted to share in the spoils of the state, assimilation was necessary. Here, Ulanhu, like the several ethnic minorities after him, adopted said strategies. Their inclusion in the cabinet allowed the Chinese government to window-dress and claim ethnic harmony. Doing so (1) deprived the ethnic minority group of the ability to mobilize for a greater voice and (2) inhibited any popular norms for *further* inclusion among the Han population. This would have path-dependent implications. Ethnic representation has become trickier since Xi Jinping took office – with escalating tensions between the Hans and the ethnic minorities in Xinjiang and Inner Mongolia. For example, since 2018, there has been no minority ethnic representation in the positions of vice premier and/or state councilor – something that had long been the case previously (State Council 2018). Additionally, in 2020, the State Ethnic Affairs Commission saw its first Han chief since 1954 (Dong 2022).

Women are similarly absent in Chinese politics. Despite claiming that "women hold up half the sky," Mao Zedong relegated gender-only minorities to either low or medium prestige portfolios such as health, gender, and education (Tan 2021). For example, Li Dequan – one of the first women in the cabinet (Health, 1949–1965) – was married to a renowned military leader, Feng Yuxing. And while Li is credited for her research on women and social issues, the creation of the China Wartime Childcare Association, where she operated as vice chairperson, and her appointment as vice-chairperson of the All-China Democratic Women's Federation, she was never able to break free from these gendered positions and organizations.

Li's circumstances were not unique. First, women were appointed to the cabinet through familial connections – that is, they were spouses or daughters of political elites. They were there not because of political competition or popular norms. Instead, their purpose was to mobilize women at the grassroots level. The co-optation of women through informal and utilitarian means reduces their ability to mobilize. Moreover, women are relegated to strictly gendered organizations. Second, the inclusion of certain gender-only minorities into the cabinet – albeit to low or moderate prestige positions – allows the government to appear inclusive. Yet, the representation of these individuals obfuscates the (1) dynastic nature of gender-only minority appointments, (2) barriers to gender-only minority political promotions, and (3) facilitates the lowering of demands for more gender representation.

Since 1979, the CCP has taken some steps to promote more women into the CCP Central Committee. A typical career track for a woman is either working in universities or gaining experience in the Communist Youth League, Women's Confederations, or the Overseas Chinese Affairs Office. From there, she could be promoted to provincial Party Secretary, the People's Congress, or the

Gender, Ethnicity, and Intersectionality in Cabinets 63

Political Consultative Conference (Lü 2020). Since 1982, with one exception (the 13th Politburo from 1987 to 1992), each CCP Politburo has had one gender minority. However, such an increase in the representation of women appears to have encountered some setbacks in recent years as the Xi Jinping administration has taken a more conservative direction. As a result, no gender minorities were elected to the latest Politburo in 2022 (Xinhua 2022).

Given ethnic assimilation policies and generally limited advancement opportunities for women – especially those without proper family lines (see Jalalzai and Rincker 2018) – it should come as no surprise that China has never had a *double-minority* in its cabinet. It has not been due to a lack of supply. In 1977, two ethnic minority women were elected to the CCP Central Committee – that is, one of the legislative bodies – for the first time: Basang (an ethnic Tibetan) and Bauer Lye Tai (an ethnic Mongol). Since then, there have been more *double-minorities* taking on leadership roles, including Uyunqimg (ethnic Mongol), the first woman governor in PRC history; Yiqin Zhan (ethnic Bai), the first ethnic woman Party Secretary; and Xiaolin Bu (Ulanhu's granddaughter). But without political competition for ethnic minority groups and popular norms among the Han men for inclusion, it is hard to imagine *double-minorities* in the cabinet as more than tokens relegated to low-ranking portfolios.

5.2 White Women in British Cabinets

Discussions of ethnic politics in the United Kingdom can be tricky. On the one hand, the country is an amalgamation of four constituent parts: England, Scotland, Wales, and Northern Ireland. We can choose to tell a narrative of how the Scottish, Welsh, and Irish minorities came to be represented in the government cabinet – that is, how the English were constrained and forced to co-opt. On the other hand, to focus on the English versus the Scottish, Welsh, and/or Irish minorities ignores the (lack of) representation of Blacks[10] (whether from Africa or the Caribbean), Asians (whether from South Asia or China), or other ethnic groups (e.g., Arabs). Given Britain's colonial legacy and the status of the country as a net immigration destination, we focus on ethnic politics from this latter perspective – where we consider Whites – whether English, Irish, Scottish or Welsh – as the hegemon ethnic group.

Table 7 and Figure 12 (second panel) both show that women are (relatively) well represented. In 1918, the British parliament extended suffrage to all women. That year, the first woman was elected *to* the House of Commons

---

[10] Historically, in the United Kingdom, "Black" has been used to refer to people of African, Caribbean, and South Asian descent, that is, to denote non-white British. We use the more current terminology, as designated by the UK government, which separates Asian from Black.

(Constance Markievicz). Markievicz, however, would not have the honor of being the first woman to be *in* the Commons given her affiliation with Sinn Fein. The distinction would fall to Nancy Astor one year later when she won a by-election. Astor contested the seat vacated by her husband (Waldorf) – a seat that she would hold on to for almost three decades (UK Parliament 2022a).

One decade later, in 1929, the British government welcomed its first woman into the cabinet. Margaret Bondfield – a longtime suffragist and trade union council member – was the Minister of Labour in the Ramsay MacDonald government. While her tenure in the government was short-lived (two years), Bondfield's appointment marked what she saw as the "great revolution in the position of women" (Bondfield 1948: 276). This revolution was not one driven strictly by women – who were a large constituency. There is evidence of White men – that is, the *double-hegemons* – championing for the inclusion of White women in more political positions. For example, David Alfred Thomas – a member of the House of Lords – requested that his daughter inherit his title as he had no son. Following his death, his daughter, Margaret Haig Thomas, petitioned for her hereditary right – a petition that the House of Lords Committee for Privileges supported in 1922, but subsequently overturned. Critically, the Committee that found in favor of Thomas was composed of all men. Likewise, the aforementioned Waldorf Astor – who vacated his seat in the Commons when he entered the House of Lords – also introduced several motions to allow women into the House of Lords, albeit unsuccessfully. It was not until 1949 that the Lords voted in favor of allowing women into the House and 1958 that the first women were admitted (UK Parliament 2022b).

And since the 1960s, women have been regular fixtures in British politics. When it comes to the cabinet, with one exception (1991), there have always been women. Moreover, their appointments are not always token gestures. From a quantitative standpoint, it is not just about one or two women. In Tony Blair's government (1997–2007), women held up to 40% of the ministerial portfolios. Similarly, the 2020 Boris Johnson cabinet included eight women. And likewise, from a qualitative standpoint, women have held higher-prestige portfolios, including the Foreign Affairs and Home Departments. But notably, on three occasions now, Britain has had a (White) woman as a prime minister: Margaret Thatcher (1979–1990), Theresa May (2016–2019), and Liz Truss (2022).

The story, however, is drastically different when it comes to the representation of non-White ethnic minorities. Britain had its first non-White lawmaker as early as 1832 (John Stewart)[11] – with its first *elected* non-White lawmaker in

---

[11] Historians dispute whether Stewart or James Townsend (appointed in 1782) was the first member of parliament of partial Black African ancestry. Townsend had one-eight African ancestry, but this was not widely known at the time of his appointment.

1892 (Dadabhai Naoraji). Yet, it took more than a century before the British cabinet would have its first non-White minister. In 2002, Tony Blair appointed Paul Boateng – an MP of Ghanaian-Scottish descent – as Chief Secretary to the Treasury. The appointment was a much-welcomed development by civil rights activists. Black MP-turned-junior minister David Lammy described the occasion as "historic," "delight[ful]," and "effective" (Kettle 2002). Likewise, Black government officer-turned-Lord Herman Ouseley noted the "huge step" – specifically, how "we are moving irrevocably forward into becoming a society where color does not make a difference. The prime minister deserves to be congratulated. It's happened at last" (Kettle 2002).

Boateng's appointment was the by-product of political competition and popular norms. For the 1997 general elections, Blair and the Labour Party recruited non-White MPs and sought to mobilize Black voters. Upon winning, Blair pledged to promote non-White talent – specifically, to let "all the talents of the people to shine through" (Ward 2002). These efforts stemmed from pressures from the Black community – who at this point were 2% of the population (and are now 3.4%). Black mobilization efforts included a campaign group known as Operation Black Vote. For Blair, engaging the Black community was an electoral necessity.

The engagement with the non-White population generally – and the Black community specifically – reflected larger societal norms as well. Labour Party MP John Cryer – a White man – saw the inclusion as a "real watershed," where he "hope[s] in future years we will see more non-White ministers entering the cabinet" (*Washington Post* 2002). Even the conservative tabloid *Daily Mail* recognized the appointment as an inevitable reflection of the country's demographic reality. In fact, it asked whether Boateng would "now go on to become the first black premier" (McHardy 2002).

Boateng's appointment – while seen as breaking the "color bar on cabinet membership" (McHardy 2002) – would further increase ethnic minority demands for more representation. One year later (2003), Britain would have its first *non-White woman* in the cabinet. When Secretary of State for International Development Clare Short resigned in protest over the Iraq War, Blair appointed Valerie Amos. Amos was one of the non-White talents that he elevated to the House of Lords after Labour won the 1997 general elections (*The Herald* 2005). After winning reelection in 2001 – with hopes of making Africa a centerpiece of his foreign policy – Blair appointed Amos to be his personal envoy to Africa (Watt and White 2003). Her subsequent political rise – and entry into the cabinet – was far from token. It also marked one of the few instances when a cabinet minister headed their portfolio from the House of Lords (*BBC News* 2003).

As with Boateng's appointment, Amos' was hailed as "historic" – one that people hoped would galvanize "more black and ethnic minority women [to] follow ... into every level of politics" (Watt and White 2003). It was a sentiment shared by White men, White women, and non-White men. Yet, aside from Boateng and Amos, there have been very few non-White ministers – let alone *non-White women* ministers since. In fact, Theresa May's first cabinet (2016–2017) was widely criticized for its whiteness – garnering headlines such as "How to Tell All the White Men in Theresa May's Cabinet Apart" (Jewell 2016). Headlines as such indicate there remains some ongoing tension between gender and ethnicity. Since 1997, the Labour Party has used all-women shortlists to select candidates for certain parliamentary seats – with the explicit goal of having 50% of its MPs being women by 2020. Similar efforts to accommodate Blacks (Wheeler 2014) and other ethnic minorities (*BBC News* 2019) are absent. And in fact, there remain ongoing frustrations with the systemic racism in the Labour Party and how it is "not doing enough to support, encourage, and represent black men" (Reza 2020).

More recently, however, the Conservative Party has made a concerted effort to diversify its image. Under the leadership of former prime minister David Cameron, the party began drafting "diverse candidate shortlists for winnable seats" (Lawless 2022). This effort resulted in two cabinets subsequently labelled as the "most diverse ever" by popular commentators. Boris Johnson's cabinets included eight women and five ethnic minorities (and one double-minority, Priti Patel). Liz Truss' cabinet was even more representative with ten women and seven ethnic minorities (and two double-minorities, Suella Braverman and Kemi Badenoch). Commentators also noted the significance of specific appointments: the four most senior ministerial positions were, for the first time, filled by minorities (Marx 2022).

The initial decision – that of David Cameron – to build representation from the ground up was a response to both the strategic incentives of political competition and popular norms. As discussed above, the Labour Party was praised for its efforts to include gender and ethnic minorities – even if these efforts fell short of significant representation at the highest levels of government. If the Tories did not attempt to make similar inroads among minority communities and supportive members of the majority, they would risk falling behind electorally. Thus, popular pressure to diversify and electoral concerns about Labour's "first-mover" advantage led to the sustained recruitment of minority MPs (Bland 2022; Sobolewska 2013), which would ultimately be reflected in cabinet diversity.

5.3 Non-Russian Men in Soviet/Russian Cabinets

Both the Soviet Union and its constituent core republic, Russia, are multiethnic federations. Before the Bolshevik Communists secured power, they feared nationalism as a challenge to their Marxist political project. From the outset, Vladimir Lenin recognized the importance of giving non-Russian ethnic groups their own administrative units. This would afford the eighty-five different national subjects greater autonomy in their own affairs – particularly cultural practices. Each republic also represented a predominant ethnic minority group. Despite ethnic group autonomy, ethnic conflict – or the threat of it – would constrain each Soviet leadership to include ethnic minorities in the cabinet (see Toft 2003). As we see in Table 7, the first cabinet had four non-Russians.

The Soviet leadership initially developed the policy of *korenizatsiya* (indigenization). It aimed at instilling a communist way of life among ethnic minorities by providing education in their native languages, rights to cultural expression, a dedicated territory, and roles in government. Such policies were essential given that nationalist sentiments were already exacerbated throughout the region during Imperialist Russian times. Through *korenizatsiya*, the Soviet leadership could both stave off ethnic minority claims for genuine autonomy and establish their ideological vision of a multiethnic communist state – all with the hopes of eventually replacing the localized culture with a transcendent Soviet identity (Martin 2018).

Part of *korenizatsiya* was an effort to have ethnic minorities in the highest levels of the Communist Party. For example, Anastas Mikoyan was an ethnic Armenian who managed to not only hold high profile portfolios (e.g., Deputy Premier and Minister of Trade) but also do so for a long period of time. His time in the cabinet spanned four leaderships – including that of Joseph Stalin's purges (Mikoyan 1988).

Korenizatsiya, however, would have the opposite effect. Instead of placating desires, the policy – coupled with rapid modernization brought about by industrialization efforts – fomented desires for genuine autonomy (Liber 1991). While Stalin – an ethnic Georgian – was an early advocate for *korenizatsiya* (when he was the Minister of Nationalities), he would subsequently reverse the policy. During his tenure (1922–1953), Stalin established the Russian Soviet Federative Socialist Republic (SFSR) as the "first among equals" of the Soviet Republics. This set off a policy of intense Russification. There were restrictions on cultural and linguistic expression; education and communication took place in Russian. Yet, Stalin also recognized the importance of coopting ethnic minorities – or at least ethnic minority elites. This was the case from the

Baltics to Ukraine to the Caucasus – places that all had a brief taste of independence as Imperial Russia collapsed. The result was the nominal continued inclusion of ethnic minorities in the cabinet.

This co-optation would nominally define Russian-ethnic minority relations in the Soviet Union until its dissolution. We see this with the numbers of ethnicity-only minority ministers throughout the Soviet period. Per Figure 12, the number of ethnic minority men in the cabinet increased – but this coincided with an almost-fourfold (!) increase in cabinet size.

With the Soviet Union's dissolution, Russia was left in an institutional vacuum: the communist ideology was not only gone but so was the union-nation along largely ethnic-national lines. In 1991, in a moment of optimism, Russian president Boris Yeltsin told Russia's federal subjects, "grab as much sovereignty as you can swallow" – echoing earlier Soviet attempts to secure subjects' continued membership with concessions of relative autonomy. Shortly after, in 1992, Tatarstan held a referendum in which the majority voted for full sovereignty from Russia. Yeltsin was able to keep the region in Russia's fold with a 1994 treaty designating Tatarstan's status as a republic (Gabidullin and Edwards 2014; Marquardt 2015). We see similar stories in other republics, for example, the Chuvash Republic (Marquardt 2012). The Chechen Republic, however, was the one exception. Following Yeltsin's invitation, they declared war. Throughout the 1990s and 2000s, Russia engaged in two devastating wars with Chechnya to keep the republic under Russian control.

The continued emphasis on multiculturalism in Russia is attributable in large part to the perceived threat of secession. Since the Chechen Wars, the Putin administration has been concerned with a chain effect of secessions – a preoccupation heightened by long-standing anxiety over Western countries interfering to weaken and neutralize Russia. Because the (varying) autonomy of minority ethnic groups had been institutionalized by the Soviet Union – and in some cases by Imperial Russia – Putin's administration has sought to strike some balance when walking back these privileges. Attempts include recognizing opportunities of mutual benefit as it pursues unambiguous centralization policies, for example, ending direct gubernatorial elections, banning regional political parties, and making the promotion of separatism illegal. An example of such a benefit is the delegation of considerable autonomy to regional heads in the North Caucasus for brokered security and often the outright repression of their republic's subjects.

The constraints imposed on the Russian leadership by ethnic minority populations manifested in cabinet composition. From the outset, several ethnic minorities were included in the Yeltsin cabinets. This included a Chuvash (Nikolay Fyodorov as justice minister), a Kazakh (Viktor Khilystun as agriculture minister), an Uzbek (Ella Panfilova as social protection minister), and multiple Ukrainians (e.g., Lyudmila Bezlepkina as social welfare minister; Oleg Lobov as deputy chairman; and Yevgeny Yasin as economics minister).

Under Vladimir Putin's leadership, conflicts have quieted – often because of repressive methods employed by coopted regional heads and the limited autonomy afforded to them by the central government. Putin has explicitly described his vision for interethnic relations: he champions ethnic minorities as invaluable partners; however, this is only for those who consider their national identity as Russian (The Kremlin 2022).

While multiculturalism is valuable to Russian nationalism insofar as it helps secure the federation as a political project, ethnic chauvinism is common. Immigration – particularly from the Caucasus and Central Asia in the 1980s-2000s – led to ethnic Russians associating immigrants with the chaos and violence of the Soviet collapse. Inter-ethnic minority conflicts have further exacerbated these sentiments (Alexeev 2010). Additionally, the brutality of the Chechen Wars and associated acts of terrorism perpetrated against Russians intensified negative sentiments toward those from the Caucasus. This has led to noticeable increases in negative attitudes toward ethnic minorities in Russia. In 2016, Russian respondents opposed their country accepting immigrants at a rate of twice the average of European countries (Gorodzeisky 2019). Note, however, that there is a clear hierarchy for the minorities: those from the Caucasus and Central Asia are held in the lowest esteem (Brunarska and Sorel 2022). For example, the late Alexei Navalny's anti-corruption platform in its earliest incarnation showcased such attitudes. He originally ran on a nationalistic and often openly xenophobic campaign, stoking racist sentiment with "Stop Feeding the Caucasus." As he gained support, he later claimed he took this approach only to gain a foothold with disaffected Russians. While he disavowed some of his more xenophobic positions, this strategy speaks to the pervasiveness of hostility toward *Rossyanie* – that is, Russian citizens who are not ethnic Russian. In short, there is a clear tension between the importance of multiculturalism for political stability and public attitudes toward ethnic minorities. Nationalism, however, allows for tolerance of ethnic minority representation – if and only if it promotes Russia first.

Putin's cabinets reflect this utilitarian multiculturalism. While there are ethnic minorities, their numbers have dwindled in recent years. Moreover, their primary allegiance has been to Russia and Putin's political project. These ministers include the same: Nikolay Fyodorov from the Yeltsin cabinet (Chuvash, former agriculture minister), Sergei Shoigu (Tuvan, former defense minister – also from the Yeltsin cabinet), and Vladislav Surkov (Chechen – former deputy prime minister). It also includes *double-minorities* such as Elvira Nabiullina (Tatar – former economic development minister now governor of the Bank of Russia).

In the Soviet Union, women's liberation was seen as a precondition for a true socialist system. Thus, under the new Soviet government, women were quickly afforded nominal legal equality to men. Reforms in the late 1910s and early 1920s improved women's ability to join the workforce by providing expanded rights. Of particular importance were those related to marriage (1918 Family Code) and family planning (1920 Decree on Women's Healthcare). Alexandra Kollontai, the first commissar of Social Welfare and *double-minority* (Finnish-Ukrainian), helped establish the *Zhenotdel*. *Zhenotdel* was a dedicated department for women's affairs, which successfully advocated for legal rights including abortion. It also provided Soviet women with guidance regarding their newly expanded legal entitlements. Such progress, however, was met with backlash as women were expected to continue performing domestic work. By 1930, the official government position was that the "Woman Question," regarding inequality between the sexes, had been resolved. Several previously granted rights were revoked. Notably, it became much more difficult for women to divorce. And in 1936, it became illegal for women to get an abortion. Under Putin – a leader who thrives on a patriarchal image and whose government is backed heavily by the conservative Orthodox Church – the social position of women continues to deteriorate (Ferris-Rotman 2018).

There are two factors to explain the underrepresentation of women – whether ethnic Russian or non-Russian – in the cabinet. While socialism preached gender equality, women lacked a formal channel to voice their demands. In fact, the political rhetoric was that since there was equality, it was therefore unnecessary to mobilize on such issues. In short, women – despite what was on paper – were not a political threat. And while the political landscape since the Soviet collapse has allowed for parties and candidates to campaign for women's rights and representation, these efforts have been stymied by a second factor: social apathy, if not opposition. Limited political competition and weak popular support for gender equality have led to non-Russian men taking the cabinet seats.

5.4 Representation of Different Minorities in Indian Cabinets

During colonial times, government institutions in India mirrored British imperial ideology. On the one hand, there was amalgamated liberalism suggesting colonial subjects would have some degree of equality. On the other hand, there was benevolent despotism – which imposed British social milieus and economic structures upon its colonial subjects. Although contradictory in theory, the British emphasized a structure in which political institutions and social practices were adapted to local contexts – including India's.

While British India was partitioned in 1947 to separate the Hindus (India) and the Muslims (Pakistan), it still left India home to more than ten ethnic groupings containing over 1800 minority subgroups with ethnicity, religion, and caste markers cross-cutting one another (Birnir et al., 2015). Hindi-speakers (as first language) comprise 44% of the population, leaving large proportions of the remaining population as linguistic minorities. The largest minority languages include Bengali (8%), Marathi (7%), and Telugu (7%).

In 1945, the major political leaders of British India met at the Simla Conference. At the conference, the leaders outlined their plans for post-independence India. One leader was Tara Singh, who represented Sikhs. Singh would later secure a distinct Punjabi-speaking state. Also in attendance was minority leader Bhimrao Ramji Ambedkar, who represented the scheduled castes. Ambedkar argued for a wide range of individual civil liberties and the expansion of economic and social rights for women in a newly independent India.

The inclusion of minorities – both gender and ethnic – in the Indian National Congress (INC) reflected the bargaining dynamics at the Simla Conference. From the outset, India had women in the cabinet. Prime Minister Jawaharlal Nehru appointed Amrit Kaur, a Punjabi-speaking Sikh woman, as health minister (1947). At the time, Kaur was the only woman. She subsequently served as sports minister and urban development minister until 1957. During this time, she was instrumental in advocating for women's rights. Kaur's activism, however, began much earlier. In the INC and the independence movement, she focused on social reform and overturning child marriage. Kaur cofounded the All India Women's Conference in 1927 and she was also the chair of the All India Women's Education Fund Association, championing universal suffrage and working on education and constitutional reforms for women.

Kaur's efforts yielded early successes for an independent India: the 1950 Constitution and the establishment of universal suffrage. Moreover, the All India Women's Conference and the All India Women's Education Fund Association highlighted the capacity of women in leadership – and gradually challenged preexisting popular norms. While women in India still face significant challenges, especially in local-level elections (Bhavnani 2009), there has been some progress. A decade and a half after universal suffrage, India welcomed its first – and to date, only – woman as chief executive: Indira Gandhi (1966–1977, 1980–1984).

While Gandhi was active in the Women's Department of the INC early in her career, she appointed a woman into the cabinet only in 1973: Uma Shankar Dikshit (Home Affairs Minister). In fact, Gandhi struggled with the concept of women leadership. In a 1952 letter to a friend, Gandhi rejected a feminist identification. Yet, she also recognized that women have a natural equality with men and that women have the ability to rise and excel at the top of their fields (Gandhi and Norman 1985). Gandhi's hesitancy toward women leadership reveals two possibilities about gender representation. The first is that there was limited mobilization to demand representation. Without this mobilization, women were not political competition. The second is the general lack of popular norms surrounding gender equity.

While both may have been present during Gandhi's tenure, a 2012 Gender Gap Report by the World Economic Forum points the finger at popular norms. India is in the top 20 – in the world – for the political empowerment of women, yet it is also in the bottom 15 for economic participation, educational attainment, and other social indicators for women (Hausmann, Tyson, and Zahidi 2012). This discrepancy highlights that it is not enough to have political competition. Popular norms matter. And in this case, prevailing attitudes of gender inequity mean the underrepresentation of women (Rustagi 2022). As we see in Figure 12 (fourth panel), while the representation of women has been relatively stable over time, it is quite weak considering the group's early inclusion and compared to ethnicity-only minorities.

The lack of gender representation contrasts the representation of ethnicity-only minorities. Singh's and Ambedkar's role in constitutional bargaining is indicative of the emphasis on ethnic representation and co-optation. Throughout multiple administrations, the INC-led United Progressive Alliance has included not only multiethnic parties but also monoethnic parties such as the Bahujan Samaj Party (scheduled castes, scheduled tribes, and other backward classes), Dravida Munnetra Kazhagam (Tamil), and the Nationalist Congress Party (Marathi). Ethnic minority votes mattered in forming governments (Nikolenyi 2016: 99), and thus the minimum winning coalition required the appointment of ethnic minority ministers (*The Economic Times* 2021). The co-optation of ethnicity-only minorities yielded top appointments including deputy prime minister, home affairs, finance, defense, and law. As Figure 12 shows, ethnicity-only minorities have been well-represented in the cabinet between 1960 and 2015.

The co-optation of *double-minorities* into the cabinet falls between that of gender-only and ethnicity-only minority cooptation. While the first gender minority in the first cabinet – Amrit Kaur – was in fact a *double-minority*, India would not see its second *double-minority* minister until 1985. Maragatham Chandrasekhar, a veteran Tamil parliamentarian, was appointed Minister of State for Women and Social Welfare in the Rajiv Gandhi government. Despite the lapse between Kaur and Chandrasekhar, the latter's involvement in the cabinet began much earlier. In fact, Chandrasekhar worked closely with Kaur in the Nehru government – focusing her efforts on important social policies. Her notable record includes the Dowry Restraint bill, Hindu Marriage

(Amendment) bill, the Suppression of Immoral Traffic and Brothels bill, and the Women's and Children's Institutions bill. These experiences provided Chandrasekhar with the necessary qualifications for the Ministry of Women and Social Welfare (Devi 1994).

Yet, there has been little reporting on the importance of Chandrasekhar's appointment. Much like gender-only minorities, *double-minorities* in India's parliament have remained infrequent – though present. In the first parliament (1952), there were at least six *double-minorities*, and this number has increased by more than fourfold since. Several factors explain the representation of *double-minorities* in Indian cabinets. First, democracy in India paved the way for demands and competition of both ethnicity-only and gender-only minorities. However, popular norms remain markedly on the side of ethnicity-only minorities – set against a backdrop of increasing calls for more representation of women. Ethnicity-only minorities thus provide the chief executive with the minimum winning coalition to form a government.

5.5 Discussion

The four cases in this section highlighted how a minority group can constrain the chief executive to dole out cabinet portfolios through two channels. One is through **political competition** – whether at the ballot box (e.g., non-Whites in the United Kingdom during the Tony Blair administration) or in the streets (e.g., ethnic minorities in the Soviet Union). Another channel is through **popular norms** – that is, when there is the recognition that inclusion of diversity is important if not necessary (e.g., among ethnic minorities in India).

And while we were able to demonstrate how these two mechanisms – and not economic development, colonial legacy, region effects, or when women were given the right to vote – drive the composition of cabinets, there was one variable that we were not able to fully eliminate at the beginning of this section: democracy – specifically, the effects of democracy on the inclusion of women in cabinets. As we saw in Table 6, the two democracies have more women in the cabinet than the two authoritarian regimes. Theoretically, this makes sense. If democracy is about a government that is "of the people, by the people, for the people," then it follows women – who make up 50% of the population – should be able to constrain chief executives to include women in their cabinet.

Of course, just because women can constrain the chief executive does not mean that women compose 50% of the cabinet in all democracies. On the contrary, the empirics suggest that the proportion is far below 50%. The fact that when cabinets have 50% or more women makes news – for example, Canada 2015 (Justin Trudeau), Finland 2019 (Sanna Marin), and Spain 2023 (Pedro Sánchez) – is testament to the rarity of such compositions. Nonetheless, the link between democracy and cabinet composition does warrant more attention. We consider this in the next section.

6 Democracy and Cabinet Composition

In the preceding section, we discussed the possibility of a positive association between democracy and minorities in the cabinet – specifically, women. There are two ways to interpret this positive association. The first is that democracy is simply a composite **proxy** for both political competition and popular norms. Consider that a number of regime-type measures – from *Varieties of Democracy* to *Polity*, from *Freedom House* to Cheibub, Gandhi, and Vreeland (2010) – code countries as democratic based on at least one of these two dimensions (amongst others). And thus, when a country is characterized by multiple parties contesting regularized elections in a socially liberal environment, it is likely to be considered a democracy. And as we know from Section 3, it would follow that this country would have minorities in its cabinet. Alternatively, we can also interpret the positive association as some distinct feature – some "X" factor – to democracies independent of political competition and popular norms. And in this scenario, even if a country has low levels of political competition from minority groups and/or popular norms of inclusion are weak among the general population, it is still possible the cabinet has large numbers of minorities because of this "X" factor.

To measure **democracy**, we use two different measures. The first is *Varieties of Democracy's* continuous 0 to 1 polyarchy measure; in our sample, the mean is 0.64 with a standard deviation of 0.29. The other measure is *Polity's* 21-point index – ranging from a theoretical minimum of −10 (authoritarian) to a theoretical maximum of 10 (democracy). The mean in our sample is 2.6, with a standard deviation of 7.7. Note that the correlation between the two measures is 0.95.

To first test whether democracy is a composite proxy for both political competition and popular norms, we run the same battery of seemingly unrelated regressions for portfolio proportions – but with two modifications (Appendix 6A). First, we include a measure for democracy – unconditional and conditional on ethnic minority group size. The other modification is that we do not include any measure related to political competition or popular norms.

The results tell a story that is consistent with Figure 6 when we looked at the interactive effects of political competition *and* popular norms. While the democracy coefficient is positive for gender-only minorities, it is not significant. Instead – as we saw previously – the effects are statistically significant for *double-minorities*.

Gender, Ethnicity, and Intersectionality in Cabinets

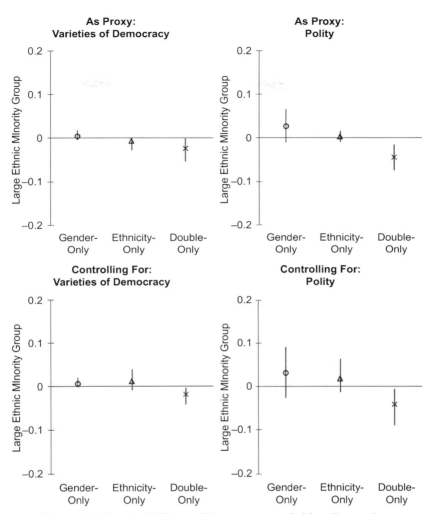

Figure 13 Marginal Effects of Democracy on Cabinet Proportions

To appreciate the effects, we plot the marginal effects in Figure 13. In the top two panels above (i.e., when ethnic minority group size is small), we see the effects are negative across both measures of democracy. However, when we look at the top two panels below (on page 76), where the ethnic minority group size is large, the effects are now positive and substantive. A one-standard deviation shift from below the mean to one standard deviation above – with either measure – can increase the proportion of *double-minorities* by 10%.

Next, we run the same seemingly unrelated regressions, except this time we include the measures of political competition and popular norms. In essence, this allows us to examine the effects of democracy – while controlling for these

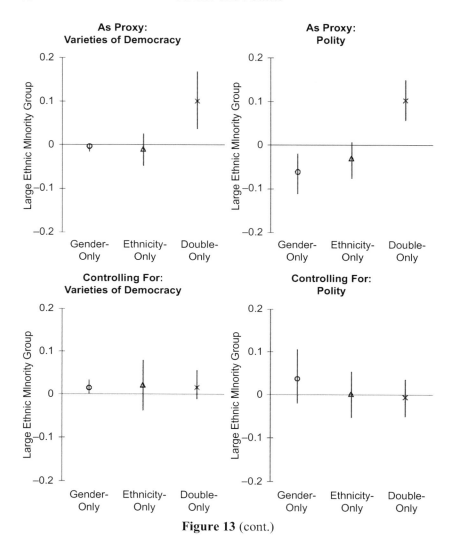

Figure 13 (cont.)

other factors. If we still find a significant effect for democracy, this suggests there is some "X" factor at play independent of political competition and popular norms. The results are fascinating. Let us start with the bottom two panels on page 75 where the ethnic minority group is small. In many ways, these results seem to mirror the two top panels – that is, democracy has (1) no significant effect on gender-only minorities or even ethnicity-only minorities proportions, but (2) a significant and negative effect on *double-minorities*. Theoretically, this negative finding for *double-minorities* is not surprising. In fact, it is consistent with our previous results: For there to be *double-minorities*

Gender, Ethnicity, and Intersectionality in Cabinets 77

in a cabinet, there must be (a sizable population of) ethnic minorities. But once we pivot to the bottom panels on page 76, the story is different. Here, we see the robust nonsignificant effects of democracy for each type of minority group. When we control for political competition and popular norms, democracy has no effect whatsoever.

What these results suggest is that while we see an association between democracy and women in cabinets in the British and Indian cases, the association is not about democracy per se. Instead, it is about women being able to mobilize and be politically competitive. It is also about there being popular norms among *double-hegemons* with respect to diversity in cabinet compositions. And when both factors are present – thus characterizing a democracy – we see more minorities in the cabinet.

These results nonetheless call attention to the explanatory leverage – and the limitations – of "democracy." While political competition can incentivize minority inclusion, the odds of it translating into prestigious portfolios is quite small. When coupled with the fact that our earlier results suggest popular norms have a larger impact than political competition, this suggests that if we normatively care about the representation of minorities, it is not sufficient just to have them represented in office. Instead, they need to be visible in portfolios of power to enact important policies.

7 Discussion: What Next?

What explains cabinet composition? We argue that two mechanisms drive the makeup of cabinets. First, *whether* there are minorities in the cabinet depends on whether there is **political competition** from the minority group *or* whether there are **popular norms** for minority inclusion among the *double-hegemons*. Second, *which* minority group gets the portfolios depends on the size of the ethnic minority group. When the ethnic minority group is small (large), it seems women (ethnic minorities) benefit (Arriola and Johnson 2014; Pierskalla et al. 2021; also see Krook and O'Brien 2010). Furthermore, when the ethnic minority group is large and both mechanisms are present – that is, when political competition is high *and* popular norms are strong – we see *double-minorities* in the cabinet. And in fact, from the perspective of the *double-hegemons*, there may be strategic advantages to selecting *double-minorities* (e.g., Bejarano 2013; Celis et al. 2014; Celis and Erzeel 2017). This of course comes with an important caveat: While we may see more minorities in the cabinet, the effects on portfolio prestige tell a different story. On the one hand, we do have statistically significant and positive effects. On the other hand, the magnitude of the effects is quite small. This highlights how much more work needs to be done.

We envision three general avenues of future research. This is with respect to **concept**. Our monograph builds on existing work calling attention to the intersectional nature of different identities (Celis et al. 2015; Crenshaw 1989; Htun 2004; Smooth 2006). By conceptualizing *double-minorities* as a distinct minority group – yet one that also simultaneously shares attributes with two single-minority groups – this monograph demonstrates how we can adjudicate between the tensions we frequently see between gender and ethnicity (e.g., Arriola and Johnson 2014; Pierskalla et al. 2021). And in doing this, we add expansive, comparative evidence to the existing research on intersectionality (e.g., Bejarano 2013; Celis et al. 2015; Hughes 2016).

Although the focus in this monograph has been on gender versus ethnicity, our classification of these dimensions should not be construed as static. While we have framed gender as binary, this need not be the case – especially as we are seeing more nonbinary ministers in cabinets (e.g., Belgium and Taiwan). Likewise, ethnic identities can be fluid. With rising migration numbers globally, these categories may change as second- and third-generations become politically active and agitate for more voice (e.g., Turks in Austria or Poles in Sweden). Who is in the hegemon group versus minority group can change accordingly.

Likewise, gender and ethnicity are not the only two identity dimensions of relevance. Geography – while it is often tied to ethnicity but need not be – can be important (Liu and Selway 2024). Likewise, sexual orientation (Haider-Markel, Joslyn, and Kniss 2000), social class (Barnes, Beall, and Holman 2021; Barnes, Kerevel, and Saxton 2023), and disabilities (Garland-Thomson 2005; Osteen 2010) matter. It is our hope that our 2 × 2 conceptualization – with recognition of the *double-hegemons* as an intersectional identity as well – offers a way to continue moving the study of descriptive representation forward.

Theoretically, we focused on the structural constraints that lead chief executives to choose representation as a necessary strategy. The focus is very much on the supply. Yet, absent is the demand-side of representation. Our analyses do not directly speak to the mobilization efforts of minority groups. It assumes minority groups want, fight for, and are granted descriptive representation. Yet it is possible that this is not the case. A group may simply want to be left alone – that is, it is okay as long as it is not repressed. Alternatively, a group may be okay with having no descriptive representation as long as it has substantive representation. Given this discussion, future research could consider how democracy and minority group size facilitate demands for representation. Doing so would also help identify when and how leaders choose between descriptive and substantive representation.

Finally, from an **empirical** standpoint, the data collected for this monograph – 91,000 *country-year-minister* observations collapsed into ninety-three countries over six decades (1960–2015) – is in a time-series cross-sectional format. And while we have subjected our regression estimates to a staggering number of robustness checks and sensitivity analyses, it is possible that we are still simply tapping at a correlation and not a causation. Put differently, countries where minority groups are politically competitive and/or there are popular norms surrounding their inclusion also happen to be the ones with diverse cabinets. One avenue of future research would be to examine and establish which of the two mechanisms – that is, political competition and popular norms – can and do constrain chief executives when it comes to allocating portfolios.

Alternatively – if not additionally – we can also leverage the existing dataset for multiple lines of inquiries. One is about the glass-ceiling effect: Does the appointment of *double-minorities* beget more *double-minorities* – or is the presence of one or two seen as sufficient? While *double-minorities* can "double count" as both women and ethnic minority, their unique lived experiences may, at some point, render them a group wholly distinct from either gender-only minorities or the ethnicity-only minorities. And when they advocate for policies that benefit specifically *double-minorities*, it is possible they are seen as a "no count" to the other minority groups. Existing research also shows that ethnic hegemons may appoint or select *double-minorities* strategically – that is, select minority women who are willing to represent the interests of dominant groups (Murray 2016). Our results lend further evidence to this claim: The cabinet positions of *double-minorities* tend to be less influential and prestigious. Nonetheless, future work could consider whether – even from these less prestigious positions – *double-minorities* substantively represent their identities. More generally, research should ask whether women and/or ethnic minorities are likely to make policy changes via their cabinet posts. And related, are they more effective when heading a minority-specific portfolio (e.g., women's affairs or minority affairs) or a more general portfolio (e.g., health or education) but choose to focus on cross-portfolio policies that have implications for their minority group – for example, women's health care or minority language education? And finally, we can also use this data to examine audience effects: Are people more trusting of the government when the administration is diverse and reflects the populace? Does this trust fluctuate given the competency of the government – for example, after a corruption scandal or a natural disaster?

References

Alexseev, Mikhail A. 2010. "Majority and minority xenophobia in Russia: The importance of being titulars." *Post-Soviet Affairs* 26(2):89–120.

Andrews, Kehinde. 2019. "Don't be fooled by Johnson's 'diverse' cabinet." *The Guardian* (July 25). Accessed September 27, 2022.

Annesley, Claire, Isabelle Engeli, and Francesca Gains. 2015. "The profile of gender equality issue attention in Western Europe." *European Journal of Political Research* 54(3):525–542.

Anthias, Floya, and Nira Yuval-Davis. 1983. "Contextualizing feminism – gender, ethnic and class divisions." *Feminist Review* 15(1):62–75.

Apfeld, Brendan, and Amy H. Liu. 2021. "Education prioritization and language spread." *Social Science Journal* 58(3):366–382.

Armstrong, Brenna, Tiffany D. Barnes, Diana Z. O'Brien, and Michelle M. Taylor-Robinson. 2022. "Corruption, accountability, and women's access to power." *Journal of Politics* 84(2):1207–1213.

Arriola, Leonardo R., and Martha C. Johnson. 2014. "Ethnic politics and women's empowerment in Africa." *American Journal of Political Science* 58(2):495–510.

Atchison, Amy. 2015. "The impact of female cabinet ministers on a female-friendly labor environment." *Journal of Women, Politics & Policy* 36(4):388–414.

Atchison, Amy, and Ian Down. 2009. "Women cabinet ministers and female-friendly social policy." *Poverty & Public Policy* 1(2):1–23.

Atkeson, Lonna Rae, and Nancy Carrillo. 2007. "More is better." *Politics & Gender* 3(1):79–101.

Baltsiotis, Lambros. 2011. "The Muslim Chams of Northwestern Greece." *European Journal of Turkish Studies* 12, https://journals.openedition.org/ejts/4444.

Barnes, Tiffany D., and Diana Z. O'Brien. 2018. "Defending the realm." *American Journal of Political Science* 62(2):355–368.

Barnes, Tiffany D., and Michelle Taylor-Robinson. 2018. "Women cabinet ministers and empowerment of women." In Alexander, Amy, Catherine Bolzendahl, and Farida Jalalzai, eds. *Measuring Women's Political Empowerment across the Globe*. Palgrave Macmillan, pp. 229–255.

Barnes, Tiffany D., and Mirya R. Holman. 2020. "Gender quotas, women's representation, and legislative diversity." *Journal of Politics* 82(4):1271–1286.

References

Barnes, Tiffany D., and Stephanie M. Burchard. 2013. "'Engendering' politics." *Comparative Political Studies* 46(7):767–790.

Barnes, Tiffany D., Victoria D. Beall, and Mirya R. Holman. 2021. "Pink-collar representation and budgetary outcomes in US states." *Legislative Studies Quarterly* 46(1):119–154.

Barnes, Tiffany D., Yann P. Kerevel, and Gregory W. Saxton. 2023. *Working Class Inclusion*. Cambridge University Press.

Bates, Robert H. 1973. *Ethnicity in Contemporary Africa*. Program of Eastern African Studies, Syracuse University.

BBC News. 2003. "Profile of baroness Amos." (October 6). Accessed September 27, 2022.

BBC News. 2019. "Labour: Groups press for more ethnic minority candidates" (August 21). Accessed September 27, 2022.

Beaton, Roderick. 2020. *Greece*. University of Chicago Press.

Bejarano, Christina E. 2013. *The Latina Advantage*. University of Texas Press.

Bernauer, Julian, and Daniel Bochsler. 2011. "Electoral entry and success of ethnic minority parties in Central and Eastern Europe." *Electoral Studies* 30(4):738–755.

Betz, Timm, David Fortunato, and Diana Z. O'Brien. 2021. "Women's descriptive representation and gendered import tax discrimination." *American Political Science Review* 115(1):307–315.

Bhavnani, Rikhil R. 2009. "Do electoral quotas work after they are withdrawn?" *American Political Science Review* 103(1):23–35.

Birnir, Johanna Kristin, and Nil S. Satana. 2013. "Religion and coalition politics." *Comparative Political Studies* 46(1):3–30.

Birnir, Jóhanna K., Jonathan Wilkenfeld, James D. Fearon, et al. 2015. "Socially relevant ethnic groups, ethnic structure, and AMAR." *Journal of Peace Research* 52(1):110–115

Bland, Archie. 2022. "Liz Truss has appointed the most diverse cabinet ever." *The Guardian* (September 7). Accessed February 12, 2024.

Blumberg, Rae Lesser. 1984. "A general theory of gender stratification." *Sociological Theory* 23–101.

Bondfield, Margaret Grace. 1948. *A Life's Work*. Hutchinson.

Borrelli, MaryAnne. 2002. *The President's Cabinet: Gender, Power, and Representation*. Lynne Rienner.

Bourne, Angela K. 2014. "Europeanization and secession." *Journal of Ethnopolitics and Minority Issues in Europe* 13(3):94.

Brand, Laurie A. 1999. "The effects of the peace process on political liberalization in Jordan." *Journal of Palestine Studies* 28(2):52–67.

Brown, Nadia E. 2014. "Political participation of women of color: An intersectional analysis." *Journal of Women, Politics & Policy* 35(4):315–348.

Bratton, Kathleen A., and Leonard P. Ray. 2002. "Descriptive representation, policy outcomes, and municipal day-care coverage in Norway." *American Journal of Political Science* 46(2):428–437.

Brinkley, Joel. 1991. "Jordanian king names Palestinian prime minister." *The New York Times* (June 19). Accessed September 27, 2022.

Brulé, Rachel E. 2020. "Reform, representation, and resistance." *Journal of Politics* 82(4):1390–1405.

Brunarska, Zuzanna, and Wiktor Soral. 2022. "Does origin matter? Ethnic group position and attitudes toward immigrants: The case of Russia." *Nationalities Papers* 50(2):219–236.

Burnet, Jennie E. 2011. "Women have found respect: Gender quotas, symbolic representation, and female empowerment in Rwanda." *Politics & Gender* 7(3):303–334.

Burnet, Jennie E. 2019. "Rwanda: Women's political representation and its consequences." *The Palgrave Handbook of Women's Political Rights* 563–576.

Bustikova, Lenka. 2020. *Extreme Reactions*. Cambridge University Press.

Caul, Miki. 2001. "Political parties and the adoption of candidate gender quotas." *Journal of Politis* 63(4):1214–1229.

Cederman, Lars-Erik, Andreas Wimmer, and Brian Min. 2010. "Why do ethnic groups rebel?" *World Politics* 62(1):87–119.

Celis, Karen, and Silvia Erzeel. 2017. "The complementarity advantage." *Parliamentary Affairs* 70(1):43–61.

Celis, Karen, Silvia Erzeel, Liza Mügge, and Alyt Damstra. 2014. "Quotas and intersectionality." *International Political Science Review* 35(1):41–54.

Celis, Keren, Silvia Erzeel, and Liza Mügge. 2015. "Intersectional puzzles." *Politics & Gender* 11(4):765–770.

Chandra, Kanchan. 2006. "What is ethnic identity and does it matter?." *Annual Review of Political Science* 9(1):397–424.

Chauchard, Simon. 2014. "Can descriptive representation change beliefs about a stigmatized group? Evidence from rural India." *American Political Science Review* 108(2):403–422.

Cheibub, José Antonio, Jennifer Gandhi, and James Raymond Vreeland. 2010. "Democracy and dictatorship revisited." *Public Choice* 143:67–101.

Collins, Patricia Hill. 2000. *Black Feminist Thought*. HarperCollins.

Collins, Patricia Hill, and Sirma Bilge. 2016. *Intersectionality*. John Wiley & Sons.

Combahee River Collective. 2014 [1977]. "A black feminist statement." *Women's Studies Quarterly* 42(3–4):271–280.

Corstange, Daniel. 2013. "Ethnicity on the sleeve and class in the heart." *British Journal of Political Science* 43(4):889–914.

Cowell-Meyers, Kimberly, and Laura Langbein. 2009. "Linking women's descriptive and substantive representation in the United States." *Politics & Gender* 5(4):491–518.

Cox, Gary W. *Making Votes Count: Strategic Coordination in the World's Electoral Systems*. Cambridge University Press, 1997.

Crenshaw, Kimberlé. 1989. "Demarginalizing the intersection of race and sex." *University of Chicago Legal Forum* 1989(1):15–34.

Crenshaw, Kimberlé W. 1991. "Stanford law review mapping the margins: intersectionality, identity politics, and violence against women of." *Source: Stanford Law Review* 43(6).

Cruz, Cesi, and Charis Tolentino. 2024. "Gender, social recognition, and political influence." *American Political Science Review*. Working paper.

Csata, Zsombor, Roman Hlatky, and Amy H. Liu. 2021. "How to head count ethnic minorities." *East European Politics* 37(3):572–592.

Csata, Zsombor, Roman Hlatky, and Amy H. Liu. 2023. "Ethnic polarization and human development: The conditional effects of minority language recognition." *Studies in Comparative International Development* 58(1):79–102.

Csepeli, György, and Dávid Simon. 2004. "Construction of Roma identity in Eastern and Central Europe." *Journal of Ethnic and Migration Studies* 30(1):129–150.

Dancygier, Rafaela M. 2017. *Dilemmas of Inclusion*. Princeton University Press.

Davis, Angela Y. 1983. *Women, Race, and Class*. Vintage Books.

Devi, D. Syamala. 1994. "The contribution of women parliamentarians in India." *Indian Journal of Political Science* 55(4):411–416.

Doner, Richard F., Bryan K. Ritchie, and Dan Slater. 2005. "Systemic vulnerability and the origins of developmental states." *International Organization* 59(2):327–361.

Dong, Xin. 2022. "任职中央统战部一年多: 国家民委主任陈小江职务调整 [After serving in the United Front Work Department of the Central Committee for more than a year, Chen Xiaojiang, Director of the National Ethnic Affairs Commission, adjusts]." *Net Ease* (February 12). Accessed September 27, 2022.

Dowding, Keith, and Patrick Dumont, eds. 2014. *The Selection of Ministers around the World*. Routledge.

Dreyer, June Teufel. 2003. "The evolution of language policies in China." in Brown, Michael E. and Šumit Ganguly, eds. *Fighting Words: Language Policy and Ethnic Relations in Asia*. Cambridge, MA: The MIT Press, pp. 353–384.

The Economic Times. 2021. "Rainbow cabinet." Accessed September 27, 2022.

Escobar-Lemmon, Maria, and Michelle M. Taylor-Robinson. 2005. "Women ministers in Latin American government." *American Journal of Political Science* 49(4):829–844.

Ferree, Karen E. 2006. "Explaining South Africa's racial consensus." *Journal of Politics* 68(4):803–815.

Ferris-Rotman, Amie. 2018. "Putin's war on women." *Foreign Policy* (April 9). Accessed July 12, 2024.

Foxworth, Raymond, Amy H. Liu, and Anand Edward Sokhey. 2015. "Incorporating native American history into the curriculum." *Social Science Quarterly* 96:955–969.

Gabidullin, Ildar, and Maxim Edwards. 2014. "Remembering referendums." *Al Jazeera* (April 20). Accessed July 12, 2024.

Gandhi, Indira, and Dorothy Norman. 1985. *Indira Gandhi*. Harcourt Brace Jovanovich.

Gandhi, Jennifer. 2008. *Political Institutions under Dictatorship*. Cambridge University Press.

Garland-Thomson, Rosemarie. 2005. "Disability and representation." *PMLA* 120(2):522–527.

Geddes, Barbara, Joseph Wright, and Erica Frantz. 2014. "Autocratic breakdown and regime transitions: A new data set." *Perspectives on Politics* 12(2):313–331

Gerring, John, Strom C. Thacker, and Rodrigo Alfaro. 2012. "Democracy and human development." *Journal of Politics* 74(1):1–17.

Ghergina, Sergiu, and George Jiglău. 2016. "Playing their cards right." *Nationalism and Ethnic Politics* 22(2):220–240.

Goddard, Dee. 2019. "Entering the men's domain?" *European Journal of Political Research* 58(2):631–655.

Griffin, John D., and Michael Keane. 2006. "Descriptive representation and the composition of African American turnout." *American Journal of Political Science* 50(4):998–1012.

Guinier, Lani. 1994. "[E] racing democracy: The voting rights cases." *Harvard Law Review* 108: 109.

Guinier, Lani. 1995. *Tyranny of the Majority*. Free Press.

Habyarimana, James, Macartan Humphreys, Daniel N. Posner, and Jeremy Weinstein. 2009. *Coethnicity*. Russell Sage Foundation.

References

Haider-Markel, Donald P., Mark R. Joslyn, and Chad J. Kniss. 2000. "Minority group interests and political representation." *Journal of Politics* 62(2):568–577.

Hakim, Carol. 2019. "The French Mandate in Lebanon." *American Historical Review* 124(5):1689–1693.

Hancock, Ange-Marie. 2016. *Intersectionality*. Oxford University Press.

Hansen, Eric R., and Sarah A. Treul. 2015. "The symbolic and substantive representation of LGBT Americans in the US House." *Journal of Politics* 77(4):955–967.

Hausmann, Ricardo, Laura D. Tyson, and Saadia Zahidi. 2012. "Insight report: The global gender gap report 2012." *World Economic Forum*, https://www.weforum.org/publications/global-gender-gap-report-2012/.

Hawkesworth, Mary. 2003. "Congressional enactments of race-gender." *American Political Science Review* 97(4):529–550.

Hayes, Matthew, Cara Wong, Andrew Bloeser, Mark Fredrickson, and Chera LaForge. 2024. "Elected officials, empowered voters." *Political Behavior* 46(1):185–207.

The Herald. 2005. "My dream to save the poor Valerie Amos was the first black woman in the cabinet and first black leader of the Lords: Her next challenge? She could be faced with halving world poverty in just 10 years." (March 7). Accessed September 27, 2022.

Hero, Rodney E., and Caroline J. Tolbert. 1995. "Latinos and substantive representation in the US House of Representatives: Direct, indirect, or nonexistent?" *American Journal of Political Science* 39(3):640–652.

Holman, Mirya R., and Monica C. Schneider. 2018. "Gender, race, and political ambition." *Politics, Groups, and Identities* 6(2):264–280.

Htun, Mala. 2004. "Is gender like ethnicity? The political representation of identity groups." *Perspectives on Politics* 2(3):439–458.

Htun, Mala. 2016. *Inclusion without Representation in Latin America*. Cambridge University Press.

Htun, Mala, and Juan Pablo Ossa. 2013. "Political inclusion of marginalized groups." *Politics, Groups, and Identities* 1(1):4–25.

Hughes, Melanie M. 2011. "Intersectionality, quotas, and minority women's political representation worldwide." *American Political Science Review* 105(3):604–620.

Hughes, Melanie M. 2016. "Electoral systems and the legislative representation of Muslim ethnic minority women in the West, 2000–2010." *Parliamentary Affairs* 69(3):548–568.

Hughes, Melanie M., and Joshua Kjerulf Dubrow. 2018. "Intersectionality and women's political empowerment worldwide." In Alexander, Amy C.,

Catherine Bolzendahl, Farida Jalalzai, eds. *Measuring Women's Political Empowerment across the Globe: Strategies, Challenges and Future Research*. Springer, pp. 77–96.

Human Rights Watch. 1994. "Denying ethnic identity."

Inglehart, Ronald, 1997. Modernization, postmodernization and changing perceptions of risk. *International Review of Sociology* 7(3):449–459.

Inglehart, Ronald and Norris, Pippa. 2003. *Rising Tide: Gender Equality and Cultural Change around the World*. Cambridge University Press.

Jalalzai, Farida, and Meg Rincker. 2018. "Blood is thicker than water." *Historical Social Research/Historische Sozialforschung* 43(4):54–72, https://www.hrw.org/report/1994/04/01/denying-ethnic-identity/macedonians-greece. Accessed October 29, 2024.

Janssen, Chloé, Silvia Erzeel, and Karen Celis. 2021. "Intersectional candidate nomination: how district and party factors shape the inclusion of ethnic minority men and women in Brussels." *Acta Politica* 56(3):567–586.

Jap, Jangai. 2024. "Can encounters with the state improve minority-state relations? Evidence from Myanmar." *Comparative Political Studies*, 00104140231223746.

Jenne, Erin K., Stephen M. Saideman, and Will Lowe. 2007. "Separatism as a bargaining posture." *Journal of Peace Research* 44(5):539–558.

Jensenius, Francesca R. 2016. "Competing inequalities?" *Government and Opposition* 51(3):440–463.

Jewell, Hannah. 2016. "How to tell all the White men in Theresa May's cabinet apart." *BuzzFeed* (September 14). Accessed September 27, 2022.

Kao, Jay C., Amy H. Liu, and Chun-Ying Wu. 2023. "Minority language recognition and political trust in authoritarian regimes." *Political Research Quarterly* 76(2):622–635.

Karekurve-Ramachandra, Varun, and Alexander Lee. 2020. "Do gender quotas hurt less privileged groups?" *American Journal of Political Science* 64(4):757–772.

Kasara, Kimuli. 2007. "Tax me if you can." *American Political Science Review* 101(1):159–172.

Kerevel, Yann. 2019. Empowering women? *Journal of Politics* 81(4):167–1180.

Kettle, Martin. 2002. "Who is the real Paul Boateng?" *The Guardian* (May 30). Accessed September 27, 2022.

Kim, Wonik, and Jennifer Gandhi. 2010. "Coopting workers under dictatorship." *Journal of Politics* 72(3):646–658.

The Kremlin. 2022. "Address by the President of the Russian Federation." http://en.kremlin.ru/events/president/news/67828. Accessed September 27, 2022.

Krook, Mona Lena, and Diana Z. O'Brien. 2010. "The politics of group representation: Quotas for women and minorities worldwide ." *Comparative Politics* 42(3):253–272.

Krook, Mona Lena, and Diana Z. O'Brien. 2012. "All the president's men?" *Journal of Politics* 74(3):840–855.

Krook, Mona Lena, and Leslie Schwindt-Bayer. 2013. "Electoral institutions." In Waylen, Georgina, Karen Celis, Johanna Kantola, and S. Laurel Weldon, eds. *Oxford Handbook of Gender and Politics*. Oxford University Press, pp. 554–578.

Kweon, Yesola, and Josh M. Ryan. 2022. "Electoral systems and the substantive representation of marginalized groups: evidence from women's issue bills in South Korea." *Political Research Quarterly* 75(4):1065–1078.

La Porta, Rafael, Florencio Lopez-de-Silanes, Andrei Shleifer, and Robert W. Vishny. 1999. "The Quality of Government." *Journal of Law, Economics, and Organization* 15(1):222–279.

Laakso, Markku, Taagepera, Rein (1979). ""Effective" number of parties: A measure with application to West Europe." *Comparative Political Studies*. 12(1):3–27.

Lajevardi, Nazita, Moa Mårtensson, and Kåre Vernby. 2024. "The empowerment effect of visible political representation." *Electoral Studies* 87:102741.

Laver, Michael, and Kenneth A. Shepsle. 1996. *Making and Breaking Governments*. Cambridge University Press.

Lawless, Jill. 2022. "New UK Cabinet is diverse in makeup and solidly on the right." *AP News* (September 7). Accessed February 12, 2024.

Lee, Don S., and Soonae Park. 2018. "Democratization and women's representation in presidential cabinets." *Asian Journal of Political Science* 26(2):161–180.

Lee, Kuan Yew. 1998. *The Singapore Story: Memoirs of Lee Kuan Yew*. Prentice Hall.

Lee, Namhee. 2011. *The Making of Minjung*. Cornell University Press.

Lee, Stephen J. 2016. *European Dictatorships 1918–1945*. Routledge.

Liber, George. 1991. Korenizatsiia. *Ethnic and Racial Studies* 14(1):15–23.

Lijphart, Arend. 1999. *Patterns of Democracy*. Yale University Press.

Lipset, Seymour Martin. 1959. "Some social requisites of democracy: Economic development and political legitimacy1." *American Political Science Review* 53(1):69–105.

Liu, Amy H. 2011. "The linguistic effects of political institutions." *Journal of Politics* 73(1):125–139.

Liu, Amy H. 2015. *Standardizing Diversity*. University of Pennsylvania Press.

Liu, Amy H. 2021. *The Language of Political Incorporation*. Temple University Press.

Liu, Amy H., and Joel Sawat Selway. 2021. "Explaining identity formation in Asia." *Asian Politics & Policy* 13(1):6–17.

Liu, Amy H., and Jacob I. Ricks. 2022. *Ethnicity and Politics in Southeast Asia*. Cambridge University Press.

Liu, Amy H., Jennifer Gandhi, and Curtis Bell. 2018. "Minority languages in dictatorships." *Political Science Research and Methods* 6(4):639–660.

Liu, Amy H., and Kevin Peters. 2017. "The hanification of Xinjiang, China." *Studies in Ethnicity and Nationalism* 17(2):265–280.

Liu, Shan-Jan Sarah, and Lee Ann Banaszak. 2017. "Do government positions held by women matter?" *Politics & Gender* 13(1):132–162.

Liu, Amy H., and Joel Selway, eds. 2024. *State Institutions, Civic Associations, and Identity Demands: Regional Movements in Greater Southeast Asia*. University of Michigan Press.

Lorde, Audre. 1984. *Sister Outsider*. Crossing Press.

Lü, Fang. 2024. "女性领导干部晋升规律的分析 [An analysis of the promotion law of female leader cadres]." *Gansu Social Sciences* 6:100–105.

Lü Fang (吕芳), 2020, "The promotion barriers and developing path for female leaders in China – Based on the analysis of the promotion law of bureau-level and above cadres (中国女性领导干部的晋升障碍与发展路径 –基于对地厅级以上女性领导干部晋升规律的分析)." *Gansu Social Sciences*. 2020, (06), DOI: 10.15891/j.cnki.cn62-1093/c.2020.06.031

Lust-Okar, Ellen. *Structuring Conflict in the Arab World: Incumbents, Opponents, and Institutions*. Cambridge University Press, 2005.

Ma, Rong. 2006. "Ethnic relations in contemporary China." *Policy and Society* 25(1):85–105.

Marquardt, Kyle L. 2012. "Stabilization and symbolism." *Nationalities Papers* 40(1):127–147.

Marquardt, Kyle L. 2015. "Language and sovereignty." In *Identity and Politics in Central Asia and the Caucasus*. Routledge, pp. 44–68.

Marrus, Michael Robert. 2011. *The Nazi Holocaust*. Walter de Gruyter.

Martin, Terry. 2018. *The Affirmative Action Empire: Nations and Nationalism in the Soviet Union, 1923–1939*. Cornell University Press.

Marx, Willem. 2022. "The U.K. now has its most diverse Cabinet in history thanks to new PM Liz Truss." *NPR* (September 8). Accessed February 12, 2024.

References

Maxwell, Rahsaan. 2012. *Ethnic Minority Migrants in Britain and France*. Cambridge University Press.

McAllister, Ian, and Donley T. Studlar. 2002. "Electoral systems and women's representation." *Representation* 39(1):3–14.

McHardy, Anne. 2002. "Paul Boateng becomes first black in British cabinet." *New Zealand Herald* (June 8). Accessed September 27, 2022.

Meinander, Henrik. 2020. *History of Finland*. Oxford University Press.

Meng, A., 2020. *Constraining Dictatorship*. Cambridge University Press.

Meng, Anne, and Jack Paine. 2022. "Power sharing and authoritarian stability: How rebel regimes solve the guardianship dilemma." *American Political Science Review* 116(4):1208–1225.

Michelle Heath, Roseanna, Leslie A. Schwindt-Bayer, and Michelle M. Taylor-Robinson. 2005. "Women on the sidelines." *American Journal of Political Science* 49(2):420–436.

Miguel, Edward. 2004. "Tribe or nation?" *World Politics* 56(3):328–362.

Mikoyan, Anastas I. 1988. *The Memoirs of Anastas Mikoyan*. Translated by Katherine T. O'Connor, and Diana L. Madison. Sphinx Press.

Minta, Michael D. 2011. *Oversight*. Princeton University Press.

Moon, J. and Fountain, I., 1997. Keeping the gates? Women as ministers in Australia, 1970–96. *Australian Journal of Political Science*, 32(3):455–466.

Morgan, Jana, and Melissa Buice. 2013. "Latin American attitudes toward women in politics." *American Political Science Review* 107(4):644–662.

Moser, Robert G. 2008. "Electoral systems and the representation of ethnic minorities." *Comparative Politics* 40(3):273–292.

Moser, Robert G., and Ethan Scheiner. 2012. *Electoral Systems and Political Context*. Cambridge University Press.

Motta, Giuseppe. 2013. *Less than Nations*. Cambridge Scholars.

Mügge, Liza M., and Silvia Erzeel. 2016. "Double jeopardy or multiple advantage?" *Parliamentary Affairs* 69(3):499–511.

Murray, Rainbow. 2016. "The political representation of ethnic minority women in France." *Parliamentary Affairs* 69(3):586–602.

Mylonas, Harris. 2013. *The Politics of Nation-Building*. Cambridge University Press.

News of the Communist Party of China. 1956. "第八届中央委员会(1956年9月-1969年4月) [Eighth Central Committee (September 1956–April 1969)." Accessed September 27, 2022.

Nikolenyi, Csaba. 2016. "The adoption of anti-defection laws in parliamentary democracies." *Election Law Journal* 15(1):96–108.

Nohlen, Dieter, and Philip Stöver. 2010. *Elections in Europe*. Nomos.

Norris, Pippa. 2006. "The impact of electoral reform on women's representation." *Acta Política* 41:197–213.

Norris, Pippa, and Joni Lovenduski. 1995. *Political Recruitment*. Cambridge University Press.

North, Anna. 2019. "Finland's new parliament is dominated by women under 35." *Vox* (December 9). Accessed September 27, 2022.

O'Brien, Diana Z. 2012. "Gender and select committee elections in the British House of Commons." *Politics & Gender* 8(2):178–204.

Osteen, Mark, ed. 2010. *Autism and Representation*. Routledge.

Pace, Eric. 1985. "Abdel Moneim Rifai is dead; ex-prime minister of Jordan." *New York Times* (October 18). Accessed September 27, 2022.

Park, Sanghee. 2013. "Does gender matter?" *The American Review of Public Administration* 43(2):221–242.

Paxton, Pamela, and Melanie M. Hughes. 2015. "The increasing effectiveness of national gender quotas, 1990–2010." *Legislative Studies Quarterly* 40-(3):331–362.

Paxton, Pamela, Melanie M. Hughes, and Matthew A. Painter. 2010. "Growth in women's political representation." *European Journal of Political Research* 49(1):25–52.

Pearson, Nick, and Adam Vidler. 2022. "Morrison was secretly appointed to five portfolios, PM says." *Nine News* (August 16). Accessed July 12, 2024.

Phillips, Christian Dyogi. 2021. *Nowhere to Run*. Oxford University Press.

Philpot, Tasha S., and Hanes Walton Jr. 2007. "One of our own." *American Journal of Political Science* 51(1):49–62.

Pierskalla, Jan H., Adam Lauretig, Andrew S. Rosenberg, and Audrey Sacks. 2021. "Democratization and representative bureaucracy." *American Journal of Political Science* 65(2):261–277.

Pitkin, Hanna F. 1967. *Conception of Representation*. University of California Press.

Posner, Daniel N. 2005. *Institutions and Ethnic Politics in Africa*. Cambridge University Press.

Preuhs, Robert R. 2005. "Descriptive representation, legislative leadership, and direct democracy." *State Politics & Policy Quarterly* 5(3):203–224.

Preuhs, Robert R. 2006. "The conditional effects of minority descriptive representation." *Journal of Politics* 68:585–599.

Ramet, Sabrina P. 2006. *The Three Yugoslavias*. Indiana University Press.

Reingold, Beth. 2008. "Women as office holder: Linking descriptive and substantive representation." In Wolbrecht, Christina, Karen Beckwith, and Lisa Baldez, eds. *Political Women and American Democracy*. Cambridge University Press, pp. 128–147.

Reingold, Beth, and Jessica Harrell. 2010. "The impact of descriptive representation on women's political engagement: Does party matter?" *Political Research Quarterly* 63(2):280–294.

Reingold, Beth, Kerry L. Haynie, and Kirsten Widner. 2020. *Race, Gender, and Political Representation*. Oxford University Press.

Reingold, Beth, Kirsten Widner, and Rachel Harmon. 2020. "Legislating at the intersections." *Political Research Quarterly* 73(4):819–833.

Reyes-Housholder, Catherine. 2016. "Presidentas rise." *Latin American Politics and Society* 58(3):3–25.

Reza, Maliha. 2020. "Labour's BAME members won't accept a whitewash." *Tribune* (April 27). Accessed September 27, 2022.

Rustagi, Niharika. 2022. "India's female representation bill is still seated." *East Asia Forum* (April 20). Accessed September 27, 2022.

Sanchez, Gabriel R., and Jason L. Morin. 2011. "The effect of descriptive representation on Latinos' views of government and of themselves." *Social Science Quarterly* 92(2):483–508.

Schuler, Paul. 2019. "Female autocrats as role models?" *Journal of Politics* 81(4):1546–1550.

Selway, Joel. 2007. "Turning Malays into Thai-men." *South East Asia Research* 15(1):53–87.

Selway, Joel Sawat. 2015a. *Coalitions of the Well-Being*. Cambridge University Press.

Selway, Joel. 2015b. "Ethnic accommodation and electoral rules in ethno-geographically segregated societies." *Journal of East Asian Studies* 15(3):321–360.

Shair-Rosenfield, Sarah. 2019. *Electoral Reform and the Fate of New Democracies*. University of Michigan Press.

Slater, Dan. 2003. "Iron cage in an iron fist." *Comparative Politics* 36(1):81–101.

Slater, Dan, and Daniel Ziblatt. 2013. "The enduring indispensability of the controlled comparison." *Comparative Political Studies* 46(10):1301–1327.

Smooth, Wendy. 2006. "Intersectionality in electoral politics." *Politics & Gender* 2(3):400–414.

Sobolewska, Maria. 2013. "Party strategies and the descriptive representation of ethnic minorities." *West European Politics* 36(3):615–633.

Sorby, Karol. 2000. "Lebanon." *Asian and African Studies* 9(1):76–109.

Stockemer, Daniel, and Aksel Sundström. 2019. "Corruption and women in cabinets." *Governance* 32(1):83–102.

Studlar, D.T. and Moncrief, G.F., 1999. Women's work? The distribution and prestige of portfolios in the Canadian provinces. *Governance*, 12(4):379–395.

Sumner, Jane Lawrence, Emily M. Farris, and Mirya R. Holman. 2020. "Crowdsourcing reliable local data." *Political Analysis* 28(2):244–262

Taagepera, R. and Grofman, B., 1985. Rethinking Duverger's law: predicting the effective number of parties in plurality and PR systems–parties minus issues equals one. *European Journal of Political Research*, 13(4):341–352

Tan, Valarie. 2021. "Women hold up half the sky, but men rule the party." *Merics* (June 3). Accessed September 27, 2022.

Teele, Dawn Langan. 2018. "How the west was won." *Journal of Politics* 80(2):442–461.

Teele, Dawn Langan. 2023. "Gender and the influence of proportional representation." *American Political Science Review* 117(2):759–766.

Toft, Monica Duffy. 2003. *The Geography of Ethnic Violence*. Princeton University Press.

Toha, Risa J. 2022. *Rioting for Representation*. Cambridge University Press.

Tolley, Erin. 2023. "Gender is not a proxy: Race and intersectionality in legislative recruitment ." *Politics & Gender* 19(2):373–400.

Tomz, Michael, Joshua A. Tucker, and Jason Wittenberg. 2002. An easy and accurate regression model for multiparty electoral data." *Political Analysis* 10(1):66–83.

Tremblay, Manon. 2007. "Democracy, representation, and women." *Democratization* 14(4):533–553.

Trounstine, Jessica, and Melody E. Valdini. 2008. "The context matters." *American Journal of Political Science* 52(3):554–569.

UK Parliament. 2022a. "Women in the House of Commons." Accessed September 27, 2022.

UK Parliament. 2022b. "Women and the House of Lords." Accessed September 27, 2022.

Valdini, Melody E. 2019. *The Inclusion Calculation*. Oxford University Press.

Varshney, Ashutosh. 2003. *Ethnic Conflict and Civic Life*. Yale University Press.

Wahman, M., Teorell, J. and Hadenius, A. 2013. Authoritarian regime types revisited: Updated data in comparative perspective. *Contemporary Politics*, 19(1):19–34.

Wang, Yan-han, Dafydd Fell, and Yen-wen Peng. 2023. "The Green Party Taiwan's achievements and challenges in promoting gender equality." *Taiwan Insight*, https://taiwaninsight.org/2023/08/11/the-green-party-taiwans-achievements-and-challenges-in-promoting-gender-equality/, (August 11). Accessed February 10, 2024.

Ward, Lucy. 2002. "History made as Boateng becomes first black cabinet minister." *The Guardian* (May 30). Accessed September 27, 2022.

Washington Post. 2002. "Blair names Britain's first Black member of the cabinet." (May 31). Accessed September 27, 2022.

Watt, Nicholas, and Michael White. 2003. "Amos is first black woman in cabinet." (May 13). Accessed September 27, 2022.

Weber, Eugen. 1976. *Peasants into Frenchmen*. Stanford University Press.

Weeks, Ana Catalano. 2022. *Making Gender Salient*. Cambridge University Press.

Weeks, Ana Catalano, Bonnie M. Meguid, Miki Caul Kittilson, and Hilde Coffé. 2023. "When do Männerparteien elect women? Radical right populist parties and strategic descriptive representation." *American Political Science Review* 117(2):421–38.

Weidmann, Nils B. 2009. "Geography as motivation and opportunity." *Journal of Conflict Resolution* 53(4):526–543.

Wheeler, Brain. 2014. "Fresh push for all-black Labour shortlists." (September 25). Accessed September 27, 2022.

Wolbrecht, Christina, and David E. Campbell. 2007. "Leading by example." *American Journal of Political Science* 51(4):921–939.

Woolard, Kathryn Ann. 1989. *Double Talk*. Stanford University Press.

Wu, Chun-Ying. 2021. "Hoklo speakers and Taiwanese identity in south Taiwan." *Asian Politics & Policy* 13(1):150–164.

Xinhua. 2022. "CV for Members of the 20th CCP Politburo (中共二十届中央领导机构成员简历)," https://www.gov.cn/xinwen/2022-10/23/content_5721019.htm#1. Accessed October 29, 2024.

Cambridge Elements

Gender and Politics

Tiffany D. Barnes
University of Texas at Austin

Tiffany D. Barnes is Professor of Government at University of Texas at Austin. She is the author of *Women, Politics, and Power: A Global Perspective* (Rowman & Littlefield, 2007) and, award-winning, *Gendering Legislative Behavior* (Cambridge University Press, 2016). Her research has been funded by the National Science Foundation (NSF) and recognized with numerous awards. Barnes is the former president of the Midwest Women's Caucus and founder and director of the Empirical Study of Gender (EGEN) network.

Diana Z. O'Brien
Washington University in St. Louis

Diana Z. O'Brien is the Bela Kornitzer Distinguished Professor of Political Science at Washington University in St. Louis. She specializes in the causes and consequences of women's political representation. Her award-winning research has been supported by the NSF and published in leading political science journals. O'Brien has also served as a Fulbright Visiting Professor, an associate editor at *Politics & Gender*, the president of the Midwest Women's Caucus, and a founding member of the EGEN network.

About the Series

From campaigns and elections to policymaking and political conflict, gender pervades every facet of politics. Elements in Gender and Politics features carefully theorized, empirically rigorous scholarship on gender and politics. The Elements both offer new perspectives on foundational questions in the field and identify and address emerging research areas.

Cambridge Elements

Gender and Politics

Elements in the Series

In Love and at War: Marriage in Non-State Armed Groups
Hilary Matfess

Counter-Stereotypes and Attitudes Toward Gender and LGBTQ Equality
Jae-Hee Jung and Margit Tavits

The Politics of Bathroom Access and Exclusion in the United States
Sara Chatfield

Women, Gender, and Rebel Governance during Civil Wars
Meredith Maloof Loken

Abortion Attitudes and Polarization in the American Electorate
Erin C. Cassese, Heather L. Ondercin and Jordan Randall

Gender, Ethnicity, and Intersectionality in Cabinets: Asia and Europe in Comparative Perspective
Amy H. Liu, Roman Hlatky, Keith Padraic Chew, Eoin L. Power, Sam Selsky, Betty Compton and Meiying Xu

A full series listing is available at: www.cambridge.org/EGAP

Printed in the United States
by Baker & Taylor Publisher Services